Koga
Educa
Manag
Series

MARKETING
FOR
SCHOOLS

DAVID
PARDEY

**KOGAN
PAGE**

For Thomas

First published in 1991

Apart from any fair dealing for the purpose of research or private study, or criticism or review, as permitted under the Copyright, Design and Patents Act, 1988, this publication may only be reproduced, stored or transmitted, in any form or by any means, with the prior permission in writing of the publishers, or in the case of reprographic reproduction in accordance with the terms of licences issued by the Copyright Licensing Agency. Enquiries concerning reproduction outside those terms should be sent to the publishers at the undermentioned address:

Kogan Page Limited
120 Pentonville Road
London N1 9JN

© David Pardey, 1991

British Library Cataloguing in Publication Data

A CIP record for this book is available from the British Library.

ISBN 0 7494 0464 7

Typeset by Saxon Printing Ltd, Derby
Printed and bound in Great Britain by Clays Ltd, St Ives plc

MARKETING
FOR
SCHOOLS

Contents

Introduction

The role of education in the economic and social development of the UK has been examined, lauded or criticized from all directions in the last few years. More important for those directly involved in education, either as providers or 'consumers', have been the profound changes in the structure and organisation of educational provision.

For the first time in the history of education in this country the government has taken powers to prescribe much of the content of education and attempted to influence the process through admonition and structural change. The latter will have the more extensive effect as the relationship between a school and its community, education authority and other schools, and the developing roles of managers and governors, begin to take effect.

The most dramatic structural change affecting schools is the emphasis on market forces in funding education through the opening of enrolment and the tying of revenue to pupil numbers. By putting the market and market forces at the centre of the decision-making process in education, managers in schools must learn a radically new and often threatening set of knowledge and skills.

There are few images more disturbing to those who are involved in education than a school competing for pupils like a market trader. Describing those pupils as 'customers' and education as 'the product' alienates people who see their priorities being ignored in the move towards greater institutional autonomy and a market-based system for school funding. The use by schools of their limited funds to produce glossy brochures to promote themselves to parents seems to be a perversion of the values which brought many staff into education in the first place.

If marketing were just about selling and promotion, those reservations would be justified and this would be a far shorter book. But marketing is about far more than that; it is about the way an organisation relates to the people who make use of its goods or services. Irrespective of whether the organisation exists to make a profit or to serve a community, as a school does, the principles governing that relationship will be fundamentally the same in ensuring that it meets the needs of those for whom it produces those goods or provides a service.

7

This book demonstrates how marketing contributes to a school's success in serving its community, achieving its goals and reinforcing its values. In Part I the nature of marketing and its role in ensuring a strategic approach to management is explored. Strategic management is the key to long-term success; it means looking to the future and preparing an institution to meet the demands placed on it while ensuring that it does not abandon its core principles. The devolution of responsibilities previously held by local government to schools has forced headteachers and their colleagues to alter their perspective on their role. While many still find the future almost impossible to consider because of the great uncertainties facing education, identifying those pressures inside and outside the school which will shape its future is essential if it is to be able to respond effectively.

Part II helps school managers, members of school governing bodies or councils and those involved in the organisation and administration of schools to identify their market, the community they exist to serve. The market is not a homogenous mass but a large collection of individuals with their own wants and needs. Marketing can help to make sense of these by identifying who the members of the market are and stressing the importance of listening to them and distinguishing their various expectations and motivations.

Part III is concerned with ensuring that those needs are met through the school curriculum. The principle of meeting the individual needs of pupils has held a cherished place in the UK education system. A market orientation reinforces that principle and enables schools to develop a pupil-centred curriculum offer in as effective and efficient a manner as possible. Planning the range of curriculum choices open to pupils so that the school is able to operate within the confines of a market-determined budget presents an additional challenge to schools which an awareness of marketing can help to meet.

Finally, Part IV ensures that the market is enabled to make informed decisions about what the school is offering by professionalising many of the existing promotional strategies used by schools. From exhibitions to public relations, schools can keep themselves in the view of the market and encourage their community to recognise the strengths of the institution and the way it serves them. School managers must come to terms with the changes in their environment and the way it affects their behaviour and the decisions they must take. Promotional activity may be a necessary consequence of that environmental change but it is only going to be effective if it is undertaken in the context of a wider market orientation.

Understanding marketing, gaining the knowledge and skills appropriate to that new environment, is essential. *Marketing for Schools* will provide that understanding and show how a market orientation will help a school to achieve its goals and maintain its values. Traditional marketing texts start from a radically different perspective on the purposes for which an organisation exists and propose courses of action which are not always appropriate to a school. Schools are not businesses and should not be treated as such. Applying marketing to schools involves understanding why they exist and adapting business techniques accordingly.

PART I:

Strategic Management

Marketing has become far more commonly referred to in all areas of the public service. In the Health Service and local government, marketing managers are being appointed and existing managers trained in marketing concepts. In education, marketing has had a presence in colleges and universities for some years; in schools it is still relatively new.

In Part I of this book, the nature of marketing and its relevance to school management are explored in the wider context of strategic management: the management of the institution to achieve long-term goals in an uncertain environment. In Chapter 1, marketing is defined and the basic concept of marketing – the marketing mix – is introduced. The need for a strategic approach to management, a clear sense of direction for the school and a market-oriented approach to management are emphasised.

In Chapter 2, the relationship between school and market is unravelled, particularly the difference in the perspectives of those within the organisation and its market. How the school relates to its environment through a marketing audit and evaluation of strengths, weaknesses, opportunities and threats provides the basis for Chapter 3, Marketing Planning.

The nature of a plan and the process of planning are considered, and the contribution an effective plan and planning as an exercise can make to good management is outlined. Techniques for market analysis which can aid the planning process and contribute to strategic formulation are also reviewed and the range of strategies (which are developed in the remainder of the book) is introduced.

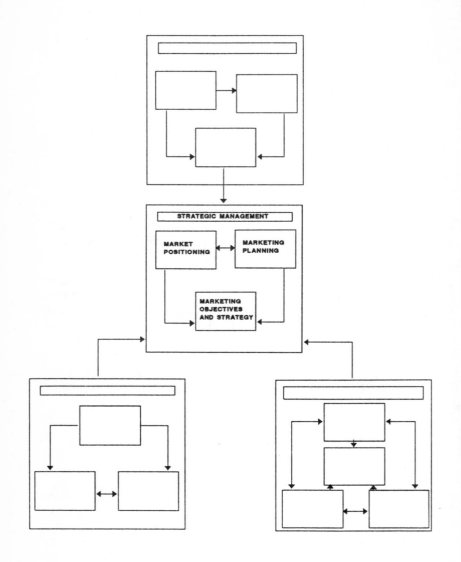

Chapter 1

Strategic Management: The Marketing Dimension

What is marketing?

The Chartered Institute of Marketing (CIM) defines marketing as: 'anticipating, identifying and satisfying customer needs at a profit.'

If that's true, what has marketing got to do with education? With rare exceptions, schools don't exist to make profits: most private sector schools are registered as charities and public sector institutions don't normally charge for the educational services they provide. But there is more to marketing than profit-making, and 'customers' can have a wide definition. Both these facts make marketing very relevant to education management.

The CIM definition stems from a fairly narrow set of ideas about organisational objectives; it assumes all organisations exist to make profits and that profitability is the only measure of an organisation's success. In fact organisations exist for a variety of purposes in a variety of forms, in both the private and the public sector. You can only understand why an organisation behaves as it does if you understand what motivates it. That motivation – the desire to achieve a particular set of goals – shapes its strategies and is the only basis for deciding whether or not it is successful.

Marketing contributes to the organisation's success by determining the kind of relationship it has to its consumers or the beneficiaries of its goods or services. These consumers or beneficiaries are what the CIM calls customers, a word which suggests there must be a trading relationship: customers pay the organisation in return for its goods or services. If this is a necessary condition for marketing to exist then its role is restricted. But if the whole range of people and other organisations which benefit from an organisation's output are considered as part of its market, then marketing has a much wider role to play.

Members of the market can be better described as clients. In education this includes the pupils themselves, their parents or guardians, their employers, the community from which they are drawn and the funding bodies which pay for the service. If you have problems with the word 'clients', or the idea of these people being in the 'market' for education, think about this: teachers, their managers, the administrators, caretaking, maintenance and catering staffs who support them, are all engaged in productive activity (which is not the same as being in manufacturing). They produce a service in exactly the same way as banks or insurance companies do. That service is only of real (as opposed to theoretical) value if there is a market for it – irrespective of whether the market has to *pay* to benefit from it. That's why this is a *market* relationship (you produce, I 'consume') without being a *trading* relationship (you produce, I 'pay').

It would be easy to call the members of the market 'pupils'. However, confining the market to immediate beneficiaries ignores the enormous range of people and organisations which also benefit, even if only indirectly. The school's pupils are its *primary* clients, the immediate beneficiaries of the service; the parents, community and employers who benefit through the participation of others in the education system are the *secondary* clients. Both types of client are part of the market being served; it is their needs which the school exists to serve.

The institutional objectives give it a purpose and define the range of client needs which it exists to satisfy. Marketing is the process which enables those needs to be identified, anticipated and satisfied, in order that the institution's objectives can be achieved.

Being market oriented

Education is not free from moral values: selecting what should (and therefore should not) be learnt is a value-laden process. How learning takes place is also value-laden: the ethos of an institution, its physical structure, its organisation of staff and management structures, the timetable, the room layouts, the type of teaching and learning practices used – all these and more affect the learning and are shaped by individual and group values. Few teachers enter education without some commitment to it as a social function, and the values they bring to their role are the primary influence on the experiences of their pupils.

The power of these values in education should not be understated; nor, equally, should we ignore the power this gives to those who work in education. The ability to define the values of an institution shapes the development of so many people. The difficulty is to distinguish altruistic values from personal self-interest. Teaching jobs exist because people need to learn; people don't need to learn just to keep teachers employed!

It is far easier to preach the importance of values than it is to avoid advocating processes which we as individuals would prefer because they cause least disruption, are easier than alternatives, or more enjoyable. The problem facing any organisation, whatever it is, whatever it produces, is to avoid becoming product or production oriented. A product-oriented organisation is concerned primarily with producing the same good or service, come what may. It might be innovative in its production processes but it starts with a product and looks for somebody to buy it, or participate in the service it offers.

How many teachers have always wanted to teach their specialism and have set out to persuade pupils or students that *they* have always wanted to study it? It can be rationalised in a number of ways, but the principle is always the same: it's such a wonderful product there must be someone who wants it! The history of consumer goods is littered with such products, some of which had a limited success until the balloon burst (vaginal deodorants are a prime example of this attitude at its worst). Other products never got off the ground. (Did you consider buying a Sinclair C5?)

The production-oriented organisation is slightly more flexible; it is dominated by the need to satisfy its production capability and will make whatever product it can with its current resources and organisation. Unlike Henry Ford ('any colour you like as long as it's black'), the production-oriented organisation will produce whatever colour it is able to produce. Unfortunately, if none of these suit you, you have a problem, because the organisation exists to fulfil its production quota, not your needs.

How many schools have offered subject choices which match their ability to staff various options? How many colleges have raised entry requirements to restrict numbers in one over-popular department while there have been vacancies in another? This is what being production-oriented is all about. There are often sound reasons for decisions – perhaps because of the problems of transferring resources from one application to another. But the question which any manager must address is: 'How prepared is the organisation to predict and respond to the market and change what we can do?"

This question reflects a market-oriented view of what the organisation should be doing. *Anticipating* what the clients will need, *identifying* what they do need, and *satisfying* those needs. It is implicit in this orientation that managing an organisation involves planning (anticipating), communicating with clients (a two-way process to identify needs) and offering an appropriate range of goods or services which they are encouraged to 'consume' (satisfying their needs).

Promotion is one of the many functional activities which comprise marketing, occuring fairly late in the marketing cycle. The product- or production-oriented organisation, however, places promotion at the forefront of its marketing strategy, as it is not motivated by an interest in what clients actually want, only what it can persuade them to have.

Where are your values in all this? Just because people are demanding a particular form of educational provision, does that make it right to provide it? The ethical dimension in education is far more important than it is in consumer-goods industries and shapes how schools and colleges behave. To suppress it is to devalue what education is all about. However there are common principles in both a market orientation and in education which clearly justify the marketing role there.

First, teaching has increasingly developed a learner-centred model, shaping the process which pupils experience to match their existing knowledge and skills, their ability and their social and cultural expectations. At institutional level, being market oriented means adopting a client-centred perspective, managing the school in a way that matches the needs of primary and secondary clients. The same principle is being applied, only the context changes.

Second, marketing is about achieving organisational goals; these are determined by the values of the organisation (its 'culture') and shape its decision-making. Marketing does not require a school or college to abandon these, instead it helps the institution to achieve them by identifying those clients for whom it offers an appropriate range of learning opportunities. However, a market-oriented approach may raise questions about the appropriateness of values (or perhaps the way they are expressed) and challenge dominant institutional attitudes which conflict with the needs of the market but which may have been rationalised by appeals to values. In this way it encourages the institution to debate and clearly articulate its underlying principles and its purpose.

Third, marketing is concerned with client 'needs' – which are not to be confused with 'wants', the overt expression of needs. This distinction is important because public discussions about education are often centred around these superficial expressions of underlying needs, rather than the needs themselves. Arguments about discipline, uniforms, exam passes are a reflection of more deep-seated concerns about developing personal, social and moral education, identification and commitment, individual development and future economic and social achievement. Marketing is about identifying those underlying needs and relating what the organisation has to offer to them. In this way it helps the institution to change people's ideas about how needs can best be met.

The marketing mix

Most marketing textbooks refer to the marketing mix and how important it is to any understanding of how marketing operates (as opposed to why it is necessary). The marketing mix can appear to be almost too simple; it classifies the key variables which can be changed to shape the organisation's marketing strategies under four headings:

- product
- price
- place
- promotion.

For obvious reasons, these are often described as the four Ps. Some commentators like to augment them with three additional Ps, extra dimensions to the product:

- people
- process
- proof (or physical evidence).

Product is one of the terms least attractive to those in education; it is used to define the service which is being provided to clients. People, process and proof describe *who* provides the service, *how* it is provided, and what tangible *evidence* there is for clients that they have experienced it. This will be explored more fully in Part III (Chapters 7, 8 and 9); at this point, however, it is important to stress that marketing is concerned with determining *what* an organisation provides in the way of goods or services. Adopting a market orientation therefore has major implications for the process of curriculum development, since this is the educational equivalent of product development.

Price and *place* are less relevant to education and derive from a model of marketing based on trading goods, for which prices and distribution systems are important. However, price as an 'opportunity cost' (what has to be foregone) does have a relevance to state education, particularly post-16 education, and the physical nature of the place (its decoration, maintenance, etc) are important in influencing decision-making in the market.

Promotion is left until last on the principle that until you are able to identify what clients need, and have an appropriate "product" to satisfy that need, promotion has little value. How you can make use of promotional strategies to communicate effectively with clients is left until Part IV (Chapters 10, 11, 12 and 13).

These elements of the marketing mix together provide the mechanism by which marketing can be used to achieve institutional goals. But before you can consider applying them you need to consider both what those institutional goals are and the context in which they are being defined and achieved. This strategic approach to management is crucial to marketing success.

Marketing and strategic management

Probably the most succinct distinction between 'strategic' and 'operational' (day-to-day) management is Peter Drucker's. He described strategic management as 'doing the right thing', operational management as 'doing it right'.

These two simple phrases provide insight into the dual role of management. Strategic decision-making shapes the direction an organisation takes and the major moves it will make to achieve its goals. Operational decision-making is determined by these strategic decisions, since they define the range of options which will be faced and the principal criteria to be applied in reaching those decisions.

A simple example will illustrate this. A school presented with an opportunity to make a major capital investment in new buildings must judge what future pattern of educational provision it is going to offer. A new set of classrooms, laboratories, workshops or studios will be there for decades. The choice will determine a whole range of subsequent decisions and must therefore be 'right'. The way in which the new building is then used must match the original design specification. Innovative layout and equipment are pointless if used inappropriately. Open-access workshops and self-study facilities cannot then be timetabled and operated like a traditional classroom. The 'right' way to use it is defined by reference to the original strategic decisions.

What's this got to do with marketing? In an educational system now opened up to market forces which must give due consideration to the present and future pattern of demand in shaping its provision, strategic decisions are also marketing decisions. This doesn't mean that the process of decision-making should be relegated to a simple response to current demand. It means sitting down to analyse the environmental context which is shaping the market now and in the future and using this analysis to forecast future demand.

In a market-oriented organisation, strategic management must start from the market. Then it must have regard to its own purposes, resources and capabilities: what it should do, what it has to do it with, and how well it can do it. But these constraints on its actions should not be the starting point for decision-making, as they so often tend to be. The starting point must be what clients will need!

Strategic decisions are the most important decisions, because of the way they provide the parameters of *future* decision-making. Their importance means they are also the ones most likely to challenge received opinions and standard practice. The ability to create discord and polarise parties with an interest in the institution (staff, pupils, governors or council members, parents, education authority, local employers, local community) can all too easily lead to deferment of decisions or compromise. Deferring strategic decisions is probably the worst of three managerial options: make the right decision, make the wrong decision, make no decision! The law of averages dictates that tossing a coin will produce more effective outcomes than deferring decisions.

It is not uncommon to establish committees or working parties when major decisions are to be faced. As a democratic or participative approach or as an opportunity to seek expert guidance or to forge a team approach this can be of great value. However, it can also lead to compromise. Important decisions, involving a choice between two opposing strategies, are not best served by inventing a third which has, as a primary objective, the watering down of criticism from the two groups of advocates. Strategic management is about 'doing the right thing', not seeking a mid-way between right and wrong.

Identifying future patterns of demand, future curriculum structures or the effects of future economic or political changes is difficult. Yet education has one major advantage over many private sector businesses: its major client group is identifiable at least five years ahead. In the late 1980s the post-16 sectors became aware of the demographic dip and started to worry about the impact it would have on demand. Yet the numbers of young people entering higher education in 1992 is a function of the birth rate in 1974!

The importance of strategic decisions, therefore, must be reflected in the 'time horizon'. Generally speaking, strategic decisions have little immediate impact. They are concerned with the longer term, which is why they must be taken carefully. Once taken, such decisions commit the institution for years rather than months, and if the market does not behave as predicted, there will be little opportunity to respond to the unpredicted.

So what kind of educational opportunities will schools need to offer in the year 2000? Such questions might appear unanswerable, yet every day decisions are being taken which determine the answers. This building decision, that senior staff appointment, this new curriculum project, that new industry compact. This long-term perspective makes these decisions more problematic as, once made, there are often few chances to alter the outcomes. The infrequency of such decisions also means that they tend to be unique, with little prior experience or practice to shape each one. The absence of precedent should alert any manager to the possible strategic nature of the decision; once made, a precedent has been created.

For this reason, it is important that the level of management at which such decisions are made is sufficiently senior to ensure it is 'right'. Furthermore, the less common the problem, the wider the information need that is likely to exist. Gathering new information from new sources will often be necessary. The difficulty of this should not be understated, but it should not discourage managers, as gathering the necessary information is the only firm basis for effective decision-making. For example, the introduction of the National Curriculum in England and Wales, presented primary schools with considerable strategic management decisions. The opportunities open to parents to select schools, and to influence their operations through membership of governing bodies, presented a major new source of market pressure. As school managers decided how they were going to implement the National Curriculum and to introduce Standard Attainment Tests, they had to be conscious not just of the staff and curriculum-development problems, but also of how parents would interpret and respond to their strategies.

Decisions like this must be made with little prior experience to go by; the nature of the problems to be faced differs from those which occur operationally. They are less easy to define, and there is frequently a variety of alternatives to be considered, with greater uncertainty over the likely success or failure attached to each one.

Conversely, the decisions will tend to require less *detail*, as they provide the framework for subsequent operational decisions. The manager facing strategic choice must avoid becoming bogged down in detail instead of addressing the core issue. Once the major decision has been made, the finer points can be considered in the light of the strategy decided on.

Having made such a decision, there must be a process of subsequent evaluation, to ensure it was the 'right' one. The importance of such decisions makes it all too easy to fall into the trap of 'post hoc

Strategic	Dimension	Tactical
'Doing the right thing'	1 Importance	'Doing things right'
Senior managers	2 Level	Functional managers
Long	3 Time horizon	Short
Continuous process, irregular pattern	4 Regularity	Periodic process, cyclical pattern
External, assessing future	5 Information need	Internal, concerned with present
Unstructured, unique greater uncertainty, more alternatives	6 Nature of problems	Structured, repetitive, less risk, easier to assess
Broad, requiring subjective judgements	7 Detail	Specific, using more detailed information
Harder, longer term: continuous reappraisal in light of external changes in environment	8 Evaluation	Easier; more specific objectives to achieve

Figure 1.1 *Strategic decision-making*

rationalisation', finding reasons (or excuses) to justify them. A clear identification of strategic aims – what the outcomes are expected to be, and when – will enable future evaluation of the decision to be undertaken honestly.

Such evaluation cannot occur until the long-term effects of the decision have been felt, whereas operational decisions will tend to have an immediate impact. It is the need to reflect coherently at a future date on decisions made today which will encourage strategic decision-making to be given the appropriate importance and care.

Eight key features (see Figure 1.1) alert the manager to the strategic significance of the decisions being made. Identifying such strategic decisions will help managers to identify how to 'do the right thing'.

Setting the direction

Marketing is about being being market oriented; strategic management is about doing the right thing. In both cases an underlying assumption is being made about the purpose of the institution: why should you be market oriented; what is 'right'? Any statement that you should do something, or that a course of action is right, is based on the values which shape behaviour and which provide you with your purpose.

The need to be market oriented stems from the economic context in which the school or college operates. Funding is related to how many 'primary clients' (that is, pupils or students) are likely to be recruited to it. But there is more to being market-oriented than this: it entails being responsive to the needs of the client groups served by the institution, and being prepared to talk to clients, to find out what the education system can offer to help them meet their needs. It does not mean accepting the free market as the solution to all economic and social problems. (Few markets are really free, and the gross imperfections in the market distort it so wildly that it is an unreliable mechanism without considerable regulation.) In education, the inability of many and unwillingness of some to pay directly for education means that the state does so on their behalf, making the market a highly artificial one. Nevertheless, it is in this environment that the education system is now operating.

Ensuring that the clients of the system have the opportunity to articulate their needs from that system is what marketing is all about. Yet the institution has its own values, shaped by its staff, managers and governing body or council – values which are important to the providers and which shape the response they will make to the market. The conjunction of these two – the values of the institution and the needs of the market – is what determines the organisational *mission*.

Mission sounds evangelistic and may grate with some, but it is a better description than the more neutral 'aims'.

- Aims are about direction but not necessarily about values; aims suggest *where* you are going but not *why*.
- Aims imply a production-oriented philosophy; they are the direction you want to go in, rather than accepting that clients have a say in that direction too.

Of course, there's nothing wrong with using the word 'aims' to describe a value-driven and client-centred statement if you prefer. Labels aren't really important, the substance is.

The mission statement is the starting point of the management and governance of an institution. Not having one doesn't stop it having an influence, because the unspoken and unwritten mission will often shape the decision-making process. For some institutions the mission is the property of a dominant head whose values and goals drive the organisation. In others it is almost a part of the fabric, the result of years of continuity in the way the place has operated.

Writing down a mission statement doesn't make it real; it has to be lived by managers and governors or councillors in the way they make their strategic and operational decisions. The mission statement should not be too detailed either; it is not about what is to be done, or how things are to be done. Some mission statements are more like institutional guidance manuals. Equally, a mission statement should not be so broad and general that it could apply as easily to Battersea Dogs' Home as to an educational institution. The purpose of the mission statement is to guide decision-making, not provide a free environment for decisions to be made in.

An effective mission statement will contain three key elements:

- *what* the institution is there to offer;
- *whom* it is there to serve;
- The dominant *principles* of its operations.

(For example, 'At West Suffolk College our aim is to provide an efficient quality service of education and training, which is responsive to the need of the whole community, in a welcoming and supportive environment.')

A primary school, a comprehensive school for 11 to 16-year-olds and a grammar school for 11 to 18-year-olds would each offer a different range of provision, for different markets, and would be governed by different principles. Encapsulating these features in a mission statement provides a statement of what the school exists for, not a detailed plan of how it will operate. Decisions about broad strategies and specific operations are derived from the mission statement and can be justified by reference to it. The absence of a mission statement makes it harder to face key strategic decisions since each new opportunity requires the school to ask itself 'Should we do this?' The mission statement enables coherent answers to be given and avoids lengthy debates every time a major initiative arises as the school, once again, has to sit down and decide what it is about.

This may sound idealistic, but it's not. Management is the art of the possible, and a mission statement which sets impossible goals is pointless. If the institution intends to offer a particular range and type of educational opportunities, for a particular range of clients, within a particular set of principles, then a clear statement to that effect provides a set of guidelines to use in each major decision, and a yardstick against which to measure institutional performance. This doesn't mean that a mission is a set of goals to be achieved and ticked off. A mission is about direction, not targets; the parameters in which the institution will operate, not a description of its operations.

Most institutions will develop a range of policy statements to flesh out details of the mission. A school which intends to offer a range of educational opportunities needs to consider how far it is going to go in developing vocational provision. A definition of the client group may lead to policies on equal opportunities. The principles governing the institution must shape disciplinary systems and sanctions. In all cases the institution must ask itself not just what the people providing the service think should happen, but what the clients for whom this is being provided think. Their needs, and their perspectives, should be given as much weight as those within the institution.

Setting the objectives and deciding on strategies

Operationalising the mission statement means converting it into a set of achievable and measurable outcomes. Initially this should be done for the medium and longer term; these represent the strategic objectives of the organisation.

A primary school has a catchment area with a certain number of rising-fives over the next five years, and sees its mission as serving that catchment area. It should ask itself what proportion of rising-fives should be recruited each year from its current base. These are its objectives.

Clearly there will be 'wastage'; some will go to other schools, particularly on the periphery, because of ease of access, sibling precedent, and so on. While the ideal might be 100 per cent *market penetration,* a realistic objective might be 80 per cent. A current penetration of 60 per cent means that a strategic objective for the institution might be to increase that market penetration from 60 per cent to 80 per cent over the next five years.

The assumption here is that 80 per cent should be coming to the school because the school exists to serve them. The gap between current market penetration and this objective reflects one of two possibilities:

1 The school is not offering clients what they need.
2 The clients do not *believe* the school is offering what they need.

The difference between these two statements is subtle but important. The first, in marketing terms, is a *product failure*: the product which is being offered is failing to meet market need. The second is a *promotion failure*: the product is right but clients do not perceive it as being right (either because they are not aware of it, or because their perceptions of it do not match reality).

Both these problems are marketing issues – though not exclusively – and there is a need to develop marketing strategies to ensure that the objective is achieved. If we refer back to the definition of strategic management ('doing the right thing') and to its dimensions, it is possible to see how strategies are developed.

The eight dimensions of strategic management were listed as:

1 importance
2 time horizon
3 infrequency
4 level
5 information need
6 nature of problems
7 detail
8 evaluation.

If we apply each of these dimensions to the primary school's objective, it becomes possible to identify the strategic nature of the issue; and the way in which a strategy to meet the objective can be developed.

Importance

An institution whose mission is to serve a particular client group, defined by its age and its location, is failing if it is only recruiting a fraction of the possible market. Raising the market penetration is important if the institution means what it says in its mission statement.

Time horizon

Five years is a long time; it reflects five successive recruitment cohorts, or most of the time one child will be in primary education. The decisions being taken for implementation over such a timescale are strategic decisions.

Infrequency

Furthermore, such decisions are not to be made very often; the institution must decide what it is going to do and then get on and do it. It should not be necessary to keep on changing these decisions if they have been arrived at properly.

Level

A decision to increase market penetration from 60 per cent to 80 per cent should not be taken lightly; it is a decision which the board of governors or council must make since it has major implications for resourcing, staffing and so on. In a constant total market it means growth in pupil numbers; in a declining market it may mean stable numbers here but a decline elsewhere. Clearly, such decisions are not the preserve of teachers in charge of reception classes, even though it will affect them and they must be consulted.

Information need

In setting such an objective, and in determining strategy, the school must research the market and examine its resources so that informed and rational decisions can be made. Most of the information needed will be particular to this issue, and gathered especially to help in reaching the decisions, rather than as part of the normal data capture and analysis of day-to-day management. (There is more about this in Chapter 6.)

Nature of problems

The problem being considered – 'Why do only 60 per cent of rising-fives come to this school?' – is of a different nature to 'How many exercise books will we want next year?' The solution to the first problem will determine the solution to the second for years to come. The complexities which must be untangled in solving some problems ensure they have a strategic importance. (If they don't, why are they worth senior managers bothering with?)

Detail

Developing strategies to achieve the objective does not mean going into great detail. The details can be left to operational decisions about the programmes of action each year. One of the great errors of management is to specify detailed actions for years ahead as if the future is easily predictable. The longer the term involved, the greater the freedom of action needed to respond to the environment which then exists.

Evaluation

'Next week we will recruit 20 new pupils' is an easy target to set and measure; but setting objectives for five years' time allows managers to forget what they wanted to achieve. It is important to carry out strategic evaluation at predetermined points to decide whether strategies are working and whether objectives are still realistic. A major new building development of low-cost homes within the catchment area will demand a major reappraisal if its implications were not included in the original strategic formulation.

Saying that a strategy needs to be formulated is not the same as doing it. But the recognition that a strategy is needed, and the setting of objectives before deciding on the strategy, are important. An off-the-cuff decision, out of context, can shape the long-term future of the institution if not given proper consideration. And allowing objectives to be set after strategies have been decided means that the institution is being driven by what it *can* do, rather than what it *should*.

The kinds of marketing strategies to be developed, and the detailed processes which can support strategic formulation are dealt with in the next three chapters. But before looking at these, it is worth considering how strategies and objectives are formulated to ensure a market-orientation is put into practice.

Strategic formulation

The development of a market-oriented approach to management depends as much on changing attitudes as it does on behaviour. It's one thing to argue in favour of a client-centred organisation, it's something quite different to make it happen. Previous sections have argued for a conscious discrimination between strategic and operational management and for a clear statement of the aims and values which shape the institution's provision.

It is through this approach to management and governance of the institution that clear, market-led objectives can be established. An awareness of the strategic nature of some decisions will encourage managers to address the question 'Is this the right thing to do?' which in turn requires reference to the mission of the institution. If – an important 'if' – that mission does enable the market and its needs to shape the institution, then the development of a set of coherent strategies to implement it will ensure that a market-led, client-centred approach is adopted.

The policies adopted by an institution are one mechanism for reinforcing this; policies are a specific statement of aims and values as they relate to aspects of the institution's activities. They enable the mission to be expanded in ways that would be inappropriate in the mission statement itself, which should be as succinct as possible. Through this, the market orientation of the institution can be reinforced. For example, policies on equal opportunities, records of achievement and tutorial systems are concerned with what the clients (primary or secondary) can *expect* of the institution and how the institution *should* behave.

The emphasis on client expectation is a clear example of market orientation since it affords a priority to the needs of the client over the operational convenience of the institution. A product- or production-oriented organisation gives priority to its own needs in ensuring a given type or level of production.

A statement that 'something should occur' is a key feature of policies; they are about values and aims and therefore not concerned with *how* things happen. It is the process of developing specific strategic objectives and the strategies themselves which ensures that policies are operationalised. A statement that 'all rising-fives in a given catchment area should have an offer of a place in a particular primary school' represents a clear policy statement. Converting that into target numbers of places offered and accepted sets the objectives and the ways that clients are encouraged to enquire, apply and accept a place represents the strategy.

Strategies are only meaningful when related to objectives against which they can be measured. It is an easy temptation to avoid specifying objectives in such a form that they can be used to assess performance. Managers are as reluctant as anyone to avoid giving hostages to fortune. Saying 'this is what will be achieved' in ways that invite others to compare the actual to the anticipated outcomes is clearly a risk if those objectives are tough.

It is possible to couch objectives in terms so vague that any outcome can be described as a success, or set objectives so low that their achievement is almost inevitable. The purpose of setting objectives is twofold:

- To provide a mechanism for evaluating strategies.
- To identify the strategies en route to the institution's aims.

These two reasons should encourage clarity and realistic optimism in setting objectives. The risk to the manager(s) involved in developing and implementing strategies lies in the difficulty or uncertainty attached to the issue. One solution to this is the use of the techniques and information sources described in the next three chapters. Making use of readily available information on the market, analytical tools to understand such information, and planning of strategies before implementation to identify problems can contribute to reducing these risks. It is also valuable to spell out the risks and identify the parameters attached to objectives.

For example, a secondary school is conscious of a perception that it is not committed to the same level of success in public examinations as alternative institutions. A policy statement that all pupils will be provided with an opportunity to achieve their maximum educational potential, and that this should be reflected in public examination success, may encourage the school to develop a strategy to raise public awareness of this policy.

The objectives in this instance are threefold: first, to ensure that pupils are achieving to their potential; without this, the policy itself is failing and any attempt to change public awareness will ultimately fail and probably rebound on the institution. Second, to change perceptions, an objective which is far easier to state than to measure; market research processes can be used but, done properly, they require resources and expertise rarely available. Low-cost and viable alternatives described in Chapter 6 can be employed but these do not provide a quantifiable measure of perceptions.

However, the third objective, which underlies the wish to change perceptions, is to increase market share, either in absolute numbers applying or in numbers citing the school as first choice. What starts as an awareness of a negative perception, leads to a broad statement of policy, and is then reflected in a general and nebulous objective, becomes easily quantifiable when identified at this level. Strategies to achieve this objective become simple to evaluate: a fall in market share, a static market share, or an increase as intended will demonstrate degrees of strategy failure or success.

It is important to be aware that an increase in market share could be *too* successful, with problems in responding to demand which might lead to poor exam results. This is why parameters for the objective are valuable – to identify the upper and lower confidence limits you wish to set around the objective. A failure of too many applicants is just as possible and important as a failure of too few.

However, the process of defining policy and establishing objectives as a result of the awareness of a problem in client perceptions has helped to define the nature of the strategy or strategies to be followed. If the school's exam results are as good as alternative schools then its strategy may well be a need to adopt different approaches to communicating this success. This could include seeking better coverage of school events celebrating pupil success (or instituting such events) – featuring the number of successes and giving results more prominence. However, if exam successes are less favourable, the causes need to be established; if the school's intake is comparable to others, it may need to examine its own performance – the product – rather than its promotion. (This is an example of the marketing mix concept being applied; there is no point in changing promotion strategies if the product is the variable needing change.) If the school's intake is from a socially deprived area then its educational performance may be good but it can still not achieve the results of schools drawing their intake from more affluent areas.

The realities of educational sociology are difficult to communicate to the general public; attempts to 'correct' results by weighting statistics to eliminate social and environmental variation are scientifically valid but rarely seen as such by the local community. Instead, a strategy based on highlighting individual success is more appropriate, where the quality of educational provision is implicit without being measured quantitatively in the numbers being 'successful'.

None of these strategies need to be adopted if they don't accord to institutional policies or reflect the mission. They simply represent the process managers must go through in developing a strategy. The mission, policies to expand that mission, objectives to clarify what those policies are expected to achieve, and the formulation of

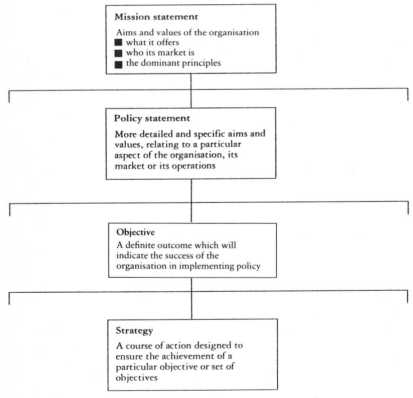

Mission statement

Aims and values of the organisation
■ what it offers
■ who its market is
■ the dominant principles

Policy statement

More detailed and specific aims and values, relating to a particular aspect of the organisation, its market or its operations

Objective

A definite outcome which will indicate the success of the organisation in implementing policy

Strategy

A course of action designed to ensure the achievement of a particular objective or set of objectives

Figure 1.2 *Strategic formulation*

strategies to achieve those objectives provides a logical structure to guide decision-making (see Figure 1.2). The complexities of determining appropriate strategies become far easier to cope with when the objectives to be achieved are clarified. Developing such objectives is in turn made easier when relevant policies exist to guide decision-making, and they in turn need the guidance of the aims and values contained within the mission statement. Together, these steps encourage coherence in decision-making and improve the probability of effective institutional management.

Summary

Schools are now operating in a market environment and must therefore be managed in a market-oriented way. This means identifying, anticipating and satisfying client needs in order that organisational goals can be achieved. Clients are either primary clients (pupils) or secondary clients (their parents, the local community, employers, and so on.)

Marketing means a consideration of all areas of the school's operations, its product (including the people, the processes and the proof), its price, its place and its promotion (the marketing mix). A product or production-oriented firm sees marketing as being solely about promotion.

Marketing is about strategy as well as operations; doing the right thing as much as doing it right. Deciding what is right means having some clear statement of aims and values: the mission statement. This gives a sense of direction to the institution by defining what it does, who it's for, and what its principles are.

Policy statements derived from the mission guide the school in the various aspects of its operations; these enable objectives to be set to measure performance and strategies to be devised to achieve those objectives.

Chapter 2
Market Positioning

The school as an organisation

An organisation consists of a range of physical and human resources, grouped together in a structured way for a purpose. These three elements (resources, structure and purpose) define the organisation physically and provide the basis for our understanding of the relationship between the institution and its market: its market positioning.

Resources

Resources consist of the physical facilities (building and equipment) and the people; they can be seen and create an image. The learning processes which those resources produce are more important, but are largely invisible. Therefore the physical resources are the basis on which judgements are made about the education they provide. The level of investment in capital in state education has created an infrastructure which exhibits major deficiencies – ranging from schools which are severely run down to those merely short of a coat of paint. Equally, salary levels, changes in conditions of service and the prevailing attitudes to teaching and teachers during the 1980s have led to problems in the personnel resources of schools.

Variations in the quality of resources and the morale of staff present real managerial problems for schools, which legislative change has made as much the province of school managers and governing bodies or councils as that of the education authorities. This may not have been matched by appropriate levels of funding, but it has allowed schools to decide how money might be allocated between different resources to alleviate deficiencies. In making the decision about such allocation, schools need to consider – amongst other things – the perspective of the market. (This is not to say that market perceptions are the principal or only determinate in such decisions. Rather, you should consider the impact that various resource allocation decisions might have on market perceptions and whether or not these are important enough to merit concern.)

A rather simplistic example will illustrate this. A section of the local population regards sporting success in inter-school competitions as an important indicator of institutional effectiveness. One way the school can encourage identification of the school team(s) and create a team ethos is to purchase its own stock of team kit. Can such a decision be valid given competing needs for textbooks, laboratory equipment, and so on? Ignoring, for a moment, alternative sources of funding for sports outfits, consider the long-term impact of such a decision on the success of the school in recruiting adequate numbers. Painting a classroom might have the same effect and benefit a greater number of pupils.

The decisions made on resource allocation cannot be made in isolation from market perceptions; nor should such perceptions dominate. They must be given credence – not treated as either crude and inappropriate or as all-pervasive and contrary to educational goals.

Structure

Decisions about resources are not independent of the structure in which they are taken. That structure represents the arrangement of resources, giving order and cohesion and determining control and accountability. The physical layout of the school and of resources within it can make a powerful statement about the nature of the institution. Formality or informality and group or individual working places (both for pupils and staff) are evidence of the school's educational ethos. Equally, the roles performed by staff and the relationships between them – including the hierarchies and power structures, communication systems and interpersonal relationships – will both reflect and manifest the institutional culture.

The institution's own perceptions of its structures and those of the market may not coincide. This will partly reflect the existence of hidden or informal structures which have a powerful influence on institutional performance but which are not clearly visible to outsiders. Equally, the overt existence of particular structures may generate particular responses in the market which are unrelated to their performance. For example, a rigid, hierarchical structure which works imperfectly and is shored up by a variety of informal relationships may, nevertheless, be credited with achieving its objectives. Equally, a school which is very successful in enabling pupils to learn and to achieve examination or test success may be regarded as ineffective by some who dislike its informality.

Awareness of external perceptions is a necessary part of market orientation. The perceptions of the market are as relevant to the long-term success of the school as the perceptions of the staff who must make systems work. A school should not be seen in isolation from the community it is there to serve (however that community is defined). The school is more than the buildings, equipment and people who constitute it: The structures which give order to the resources are equally important to the achievement of institutional goals.

All too often schools operate like the military, having an officer cadre (the teaching staff) and 'other ranks' (the non-teaching or support staff). This two-class division can be of little significance in small institutions, but in larger ones it can be a powerful inhibiting factor in 'internal marketing'.

Internal marketing refers to the process of influencing staff within the institution to support particular strategies and to operate systems and procedures in a way which enables aims and objectives to be achieved. For example, a strategy to encourage parental participation in learning by inviting parents into classrooms is going to be ineffective (counter productive even) if individual members of staff are unwilling to support the policy.

Why is this of particular concern in relation to non-teaching staff? The designation of such staff by what they *don't* do (ie teach) is a reflection of the problem. All too often such staff are undervalued or disregarded, expected to fit their work patterns into those of teaching staff. All too often they can be regarded as dispensable when resources are tight.

Such staff may be the first point of contact between the school and its market. Their ability to get appropriate responses from other staff, or their attitude to callers or visitors, is thus a crucial reflection of the school.

Purpose

Purpose is the most important organisational dimension since it should be the *unifying* one. 'Purpose' has already been discussed in Chapter 1, as it is expressed through the organisation's aims or mission. However, when considering how an institution's mission affects its operations it is important to recognise the effect of its organisational culture. This is a difficult concept to define since it lacks any direct physical expression, in the way that institutional aims can be written down as a mission statement. Nevertheless, a culture exists in every organisation and is an essential element of the way resources are used and the organisational structure functions.

Culture can most clearly be seen in the relationships which exist between staff:

- formality/informality (of interpersonal relationships)
- formality/informality (of organisational systems)
- departmental identification/institutional identification.

It can also be seen in the extent to which all staff are committed to institutional aims. This will be reflected in the way that their individual and group performance are motivated by a desire to achieve objectives deriving from those aims.

Culture may only be a subjectively observable phenomenon, but it can be very powerful in determining how effective the school's resources and organisational structures are. Culture reflects the motivation of staff to overcome deficiencies or, when there is a high standard of resourcing and a well-organised institution, the 'spark' which is needed for a full-hearted pursuit of the school's goals. (One of the features of organisations with charismatic leaders has been found to be their success in ensuring the identification of staff with the organisation's goals.)

Appropriate culture, then, is a necessary pre-condition for the effective pursuit of organisational purpose – but it is not a sufficient one. The nature of the organisation's resource base and the structures arranging and uniting those resources are crucial to for long-term success, and to a match between the organisation and its environment.

Image and reality

The image the organisation presents to the market is a product of these organisational dimensions, but the image is intermediated in the perceptions of the market by its members' own expectations and experiences. It is the relationship between image and reality which needs to be appreciated if educational managers are to ensure that the image held by the market matches their ability to deliver. In later chapters, particularly Chapter 12, the techniques for managing the institution's image will be explored in more detail. At this stage it is important to establish the nature of the relationship between image and reality.

We all perceive reality in different ways, as a result of the socialisation process which makes us able to make sense of the various phenomena we encounter. The experiences we all have as children encourage us to develop certain beliefs about education in general. Added to these personal experiences are the effects of our various political and social beliefs and the factors which shape them.

By definition, those who work in education will have experiences which differentiate them from those who don't. These are a product of the values and attitudes which cause people to enter teaching, and the day-to-day experiences resulting from that decision.

The 'reality' of a school may appear very different to those outside the organisation than to those within. This perception results from a range of direct and indirect forms of contact with the school, such as:

- personal contact (visiting the school, telephoning or corresponding with it, and so on);
- impersonal contact (through the various media by which information and publicity are communicated);
- direct or hearsay experience of the school (as former pupils, for example);
- direct or hearsay experience of the school's operations (by, for example, the way it deals with personal contacts, encourages parental participation, uses open days, and so on)
- behaviour of its staff and pupils (both inside and outside the school);
- size, age and structure of the school;
- nature of the curricular offer (not just the diversity of subject offerings, but also the variety of learning experiences available);

- historical performance (particularly examination successes, where appropriate, and the quality of education provided, according to the measures of quality used by the perceiver);
- institutional visibility (including ability to project image and performance effectively: see Chapter 12).

Within this list of features you may notice how little mention is made of those aspects of the institutional image usually associated with marketing, such as publicity materials. In later chapters there will be plenty of opportunity to explore how such materials can contribute to a positive image for the school. However, it is important to stress that the market's images of the school result from a variety of points of contact with the institution; without some consistency in those experiences, no amount of publicity will counter the mixed messages being sent out.

Furthermore, general images of schools which are projected through the media are totally beyond the control of any single institution, yet each is affected by them. Given the tendency of the mass media to simplify complex issues and to emphasise disaster rather than stability, there is a constant stream of images about schools being projected which the individual school must recognise. Furthermore, the ability of individuals to hold conflicting images simultaneously makes it even more difficult to influence perception. For example, it is possible for individuals to criticise the performance of a particular category of institution or institutional activity, while expressing satisfaction with an individual school in that category or which undertakes such activity. Equally, support for such categories or activities in general may be expressed while a particular example is condemned for its participation in that category or activity. (For example, people will agree with the proposition that very small schools are economically unviable and that rationalisation of provision is sensible, but argue passionately for the retention of a local small school.)

Such conflicting behaviour exemplifies the power of beliefs over experience. In trying to project a particular image, a manager needs to recognise that changing powerfully held beliefs is beyond the resources available. It may only be possible to dent prejudice or to encourage an element of doubt where once there was certainty.

Whether the market's views are initially seen as positive or negative, the school can only ensure that it projects a consistent image if it concentrates on all aspects of its interaction with the environment and encourages all its staff to support that image through their everyday practice. A thousand positive experiences can be undone by a single negative one. It is claimed that in commercial organisations only 1 per cent of customers complain about bad service or products, but that only 10 per cent of those having such a bad experience will buy again. It is worth considering how often a failure by the school to perform in the way it should (to conform to its desired image) has led to a complaint, and how often such an experience has led to complaints to others but not the school. Ultimately, the school must ensure that the reality of its performance reflects the image it wishes to project, and not just accept the image it projects because of the reality it allows to exist.

The school's position

'Positioning' is a term used to describe the way in which an organisation relates to its market. Primarily it is about constructing an image, or influencing the image held of the organisation, so that its market relationship occurs in a particular way, and it is perceived as operating in a particular market sector or niche.

A simple example, from retailing. From its inception, the store group Tesco relied on extreme price competitiveness to attract custom. The decor and facilities in its shops illustrated this, being very utilitarian, and the staff levels were kept to the barest minimum. The motto of Jack Cohen, the company's founder, was 'pile them high and sell them cheap'.

Such an approach had a number of consequences. It created a powerful image which was reinforced every time someone visited a Tesco store, and encouraged the association of the name with various other concepts. Low price is not the only meaning of cheap. It also suggests shoddy, low-quality goods, and is associated with images of poor taste and low income.

Increasingly, Tesco found its market share being confined to lower-income groups while competitors such as Sainsbury expanded market share by appealing to the more affluent population sectors, which were in the majority. From the late 1970s and throughout the 1980s Tesco set out on a deliberate policy of image change, by upgrading stores and introducing new product lines. It has been a long and slow process which suffers from a major problem: persuading potential customers to try the 'new' Tesco stores and experience the changed operations does not, in itself, change the image which is held. The ability to experience one type of reality and to hold an image of another is what makes repositioning such a time-consuming and expensive operation.

A school's market position is the result of stereotypical images held by the market and the effect of the various forms of contact outlined in the previous section. The school will tend to be categorised as fitting into a particular category which may bear very little relationship to the reality of that or any other school.

A small, 50-pupil village school will be seen by many potential parents as friendly, relaxed and welcoming. It may also be thought a bit old-fashioned, under-resourced and limited in the range of learning experiences or specialisms of its teachers. Such an image may well stem as much from a TV series about a 1930s mining community as from the reality of a primary school in the 1990s! Similarly, images will exist for a 1500-pupil comprehensive school, a 500-pupil grammar school, and so on. The school starts off positioned according to stereotypical images.

The school needs to define for itself how it wishes to be perceived and what place in the market it wishes to fill. It should not be assumed that stereotypes can be changed simply by creating a different reality, nor should such stereotypes be ignored because they are unrelated to reality or the result of prejudice. Images can only be changed by starting from where the market is, and encouraging it to shift its perception.

A school which is seen as providing a high-quality education for the 'academic' minority but offering and/or caring little about the majority (perhaps an ex-grammar turned comprehensive) may wish to reposition itself by convincing the market of its genuine commitment to the whole range of aptitudes and abilities. It needs to examine all aspects of its institutional behaviour, of its interface with the public and the various images which that public holds. Above all it must ensure that the image it wishes to project is the reality of the school. Otherwise it is better for such an institution to concentrate on a 'niche' market (a small, specialist sector of the whole market) which it is capable of supplying effectively.

Repositioning a school, ensuring that the reality is what it should be and that perceptions of it reflect that policy, is neither easy nor quick.

Given the resource limitations facing schools, changes in institutional performance and the use of various forms of promotion and publicity to create new perceptions will only have effect over the medium to long term.

In Chapter 12, techniques for image creation and image change are explored in detail. However, before embarking on a market repositioning strategy, a school must be certain where it is starting from and where it is going.

The marketing audit

The need to establish the school's present position in the market involves a marketing audit of the institution and the environment in which it operates. An audit is a critical appraisal of both these dimensions and is often difficult to undertake when the auditors are themselves part of the institution. Nevertheless, being aware of the subjectivity which is unsuitable in such an exercise doesn't prevent participants from questioning received opinion and behaviour which normally goes unchallenged.

An audit can be divided into two components:

- an *internal* audit of marketing resources and activities; and
- an *external* audit of the market environment in which the school is operating.

Following an audit, the data collected must be evaluated and conclusions about the school and its market arrived at. This will enable coherent decisions to be taken regarding the market position and the strategic options open to the school.

Internal audit

The internal audit should start by identifying existing marketing objectives – either explicit or implicit – which shape existing strategies. What is the school currently setting out to achieve in its marketing activity? If such objectives have not been clearly spelt out there may be indications of the general goals shaping marketing in the kinds of strategy being adopted.

The second area for investigation is institutional performance in the marketplace. The most obvious indicator is numbers enrolled at the school, but it is also possible to include such indicators as numbers enquiring, the number of favourable (or unfavourable) mentions in local press, the development of links or work-experience placements with local employers, and so on. Clearly, performance in the market cross-refers to marketing objectives, but making judgements or arriving at conclusions about effectiveness should be avoided until the audit is completed.

Having identified objectives and performance, the third area for auditing is the way in which marketing is organised – and the responsibilities for marketing activity. Questions need to be asked about who undertakes marketing activity, what they do, how and when it is done. The responsibility for marketing budgets and budgetary control systems should also be explored.

All too often the major interface between an organisation and its market receives the least attention. School secretaries may see more potential parents than anyone else in the school, yet they may have received little or no training or guidance; parents evenings may be given a low priority as a marketing event with the result that an opportunity to raise the institutional profile may be lost in the need to undertake a major logistical exercise.

The fourth and final area to explore is the product of this marketing organisation: the marketing materials and operations and their outcomes. An assessment should be made of the school's image in the market, identifying how people perceive the institution. The nature and quality of any promotional or publicity material needs to be examined and its effectiveness judged. The various activities undertaken by the school which are designed to attract market interest – open days or evenings, school fetes, sporting events, and the like – should be evaluated. (As will be seen later, simple methods can be used to capture the most important perceptions, those of the market.)

It is too easy to treat the internal audit as a purely nominal activity; after all, for those working in a school much of this information is so readily available as not to seem worth collecting formally. Nevertheless there are advantages in making the audit a specific exercise, both to emphasise its importance and also to identify marketing data and activities which may not otherwise be considered. (See Figure 2.1)

External audit

The external audit is concerned with the environment in which the

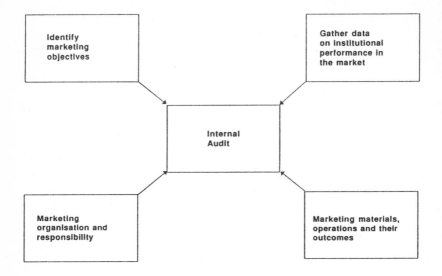

Figure 2.1 *The Internal Audit*

school is operating and includes all those details of the market which have an impact on the decision whether or not to respond positively to the school's marketing effort.

The most obvious aspect of the market is its size and location – the geodemographics. This will start from basic data, such as the forecast for the next few years of the number of rising-fives or rising-elevens (or whatever age group the school recruits from). This will need to take account of migration patterns, housing developments and so on.

The *socio-cultural* features of this population should also be considered – ethnicity, religion, employment, housing tenancy and so on – will all have an impact on market decisions. It is obvious to highlight the differences between inner city and suburban populations, a multi-ethnic urban area and a predominantly white, rural area. But in analysing the market, care must be taken not to ignore the total population by focusing on the existing rather than potential market. A particular group or sub-group within the catchment area may have gone unnoticed due to a failure to communicate in the past. A careful analysis of the population characteristics, of changes in the past and projected changes in the future, is an essential element of the external audit. (Much of this data can be obtained from the education authority's own research or statistics section, or from the planning or economic development departments.)

The local employment market should also be examined, as the long-term impact of pupils' and parents' employment expectations will affect their expectations about schools. Also, schools are increasingly looking to employers to provide work experience, to assist in project work or to participate in compacts. A careful analysis of current employment, and of changes occurring in the employment market can contribute to a better understanding of the external demands being placed on the school. (Again, such data can be obtained from the education authority, planning or economic development departments.)

The fourth aspect of the environment to be included in the external audit is the 'competition' – the number and nature of alternative providers, in both the public and private sectors. Education is not about fighting over pupils and attempting to score points; least of all is it about making unfavourable comparisons between other institutions and a manager's own, in the hope of benefiting. Nevertheless, it is important to know the choices open to parents and their children, to enable a school to decide how far it wants to differentiate itself, and to help it to understand the factors including decisions.

The political and legislative environment, at both local or national government level, is a key feature of a school's market. The level of funding, the regulations and policies affecting provision, the expectations placed on the school – all have a major impact on its strategies and operations. These are part of the market environment and should be analysed; the underlying principles and pressures shaping them must be considered if the school is to understand how its future is being determined.

In particular, this aspect of the environment determines the range of options open to the school in its marketing objectives, its curriculum provision, its capital resources and the powers residing in the school and its education authority.

The labour market in which the school has to compete has had a dramatic impact in the last few years on the way schools are able to respond to the market. The ability to recruit staff with appropriate skills (or to recruit any staff) determines both how the school can shape its provision and how it will be perceived. For some schools the

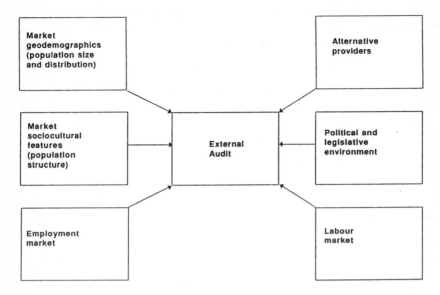

Figure 2.2 *The External Audit*

existence of high local housing costs discourages teachers from applying; the problems this creates can have both positive and negative results. Parents can be put off by the fear that a school is not able to offer an adequate curriculum; alternatively, they have been known to offer access to low-cost housing to encourage job applicants. The analysis of this and the other external characteristics enables the school to identify the environment in which it is operating (see Figure 2.2).

Carrying out the audit – both internal and external – can be an ideal opportunity to encourage staff awareness of the importance of the market in determining the school's future strategies. It is a valuable exercise in its own right, to collect the data, but this value can be increased by carrying out a two-stage staff development exercise.

Stage one of this exercise involves identifying the areas for audit and allocating responsibility for collecting and analysing the data. the individuals or groups then plan the timescale and identify sources to enable them to undertake their part of the audit. Stage two of the exercise involves presentation and analysis of this data. As a group exercise staff will begin to appreciate not only how important marketing is to the school but also the importance of each member of staff to the school's marketing stance. In particular they will find that the evaluation of the audit data requires them to agree a range of criteria for making judgements about the school and its environment.

Evaluating the audit: SWOT analysis

A number of mechanisms are available to assist in the evaluation of market data: management textbooks are full of models for strategic analysis. Chapter 3 explains a number of these and evaluates their effectiveness to school managers. The purpose of the evaluation is to identify how the school relates to its market, by examining the school's own marketing and the market in which it operates. This helps to define the school's market position. The simplest and most widely used technique which is particularly applicable as a mechanism for evaluating the marketing audit in SWOT analysis.

SWOT stands for:

- strengths;
- weaknesses;
- opportunities;
- threats.

Strengths and weaknesses

Strengths and weaknesses arise within the organisation and are therefore appropriate for evaluating the internal audit. Strengths will be identified as those features of the school's performance in the market or of the school's marketing operations which are judged to be successful. Clearly, in making these judgements there must be some criteria for categorizing performance; these need to be clearly articulated.

For example, a school which decided to set the objective of an increase in the number of 16-year-olds staying on in the sixth form might judge an improvement in staying-on as a marketing success. However, the criterion for judging success (an increase in staying-on rates) might have been set differently. The criterion could have been a 28 per cent staying on rate and performance judged a failure (reflecting an underlying weakness) if the target rate had not been achieved (say an increase to only 25 per cent). If the staying on rate attained was still below national, local or geographically comparable staying-on rates, then this too would indicate a weakness if the comparable rates were being used as the criterion.

Thus judgements about strengths and weaknesses require important questions to be asked about how those judgements are to be arrived at. It is this feature of the evaluation which is as valuable as the analysis of the data on the school. Clearly there is a substantial element of subjectivity in the evaluation and it is the debate which is generated in arriving at conclusions about strengths and weaknesses which enables consensus to emerge about areas for development (to build on strengths) and areas for change (to overcome weaknesses).

Conflicting conclusions might also occur. For example, a school may judge that its success in attracting children from its catchment area (a high market penetration) arises from the strength of its relationship with the community. This may include the widespread use of school facilities for community activities (adult education, drama groups, youth clubs, and so on). Conversely, a failure to generate extra income from the use of facilities for out-of-school activities may be seen as a weakness. However, the weakness may arise from charging low or no fees to the community to encourage the widest possible use, thus generating a high institutional profile and the consequent high market penetration for its major purpose, as a school.

Should the school develop the use of the school further to build on its strength as a community focus with the consequent high level of recruitment, or should it change its policy on pricing to increase revenue at the risk of discouraging some users? It is through the debate which this generates that coherent decisions are arrived at. The judgements being made are clearly subjective but the data on which judgements are made comes from the internal audit and provides a firm basis for those judgements.

Opportunities and Threats

Opportunities and threats arise outside the organisation from the environment in which it operates. As the example above showed, strengths and weaknesses can often arise from the same cause; the same is true of opportunities and threats. Just as a bottle of milk can be half full or half empty, so a feature of the environment can be thought of as an opportunity or as a threat. Once again a simple example may illustrate this.

The introduction of the National Curriculum imposed a substantial burden on schools and forced many to reconsider how possible it would be to continue to offer unconventional subjects or patterns of provision. Thus the National Curriculum has seemed to threaten features of the school which were perceived as strengths. However, if it is possible to rearrange the curriculum structure to enable such provision to be continued within the National Curriculum, that then becomes an opportunity to demonstrate the validity of the school's particular offer. Clearly this will not always be the case; a school which has promoted music or science and given over a higher than average amount of the school week to that area of the curriculum may find the National Curriculum has been a major threat to this particular strategy. The impact on the school's marketing of the National Curriculum needs to be considered as it must judge how much of its recruitment derived from the particular curriculum strategy it pursued.

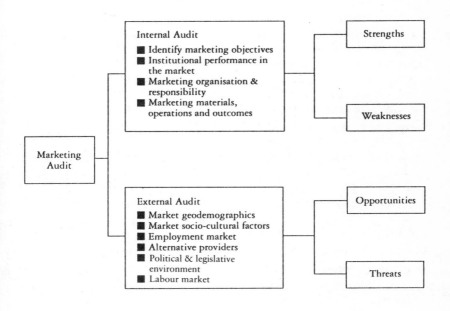

Figure 2.3 *'Where are we now?'*

SWOT outcomes

The outcomes of the SWOT analysis help define the school's present position in the market; they question 'Where are we now?'

The questions the school then has to ask itself concern the objectives it wishes to set for itself ('Where are we going?') and the strategies which will enable it to achieve these objectives ('How do we get there?'). Together, these three questions provide the framework for the institution's marketing plan (see Figure 2.3)

Summary

The school is a set of resources, organised in a particular way to achieve a particular purpose. How well it does this depends on the quality and quantity of those resources, the effectiveness of that organisation structure and of the culture of the organisation in linking the elements together and motivating its staff.

The reality of the school and the image of it in the market are not necessarily the same. Perception is determined by individuals' experiences, beliefs and values and the reality may not fit these images; but that does not prevent people from having distorted perceptions to fit their expectations.

A school's position in the market reflects its relationship to the market: the image the market holds of it in relation to a set of stereotypes. Determining market position through a marketing audit involves identifying marketing objectives, performance, organisation and responsibility, and operations (the internal audit). This is then contrasted with the external audit, the market geodemographics, its socio-cultural and politico-legislative environment, its labour and employment markets and its competition.

The analysis of these audits, the identification of strengths and weaknesses, opportunities and threats, enables the school to identify its market position. It must then go on to relate that to its objectives in defining future marketing strategies.

Chapter 3
Planning Your Marketing

What is the point of planning?

Nothing in life is predictable – except its unpredictability! We are constantly warned that plans are bound to be upset by the uncertainties that bedevil our lives, and that we would do better to prepare ourselves to deal with each as it occurs. Yet if that were true we should resign ourselves to a state of constant anxiety about what is to happen tomorrow.

Clearly, the need to prepare for the future is a part of any manager's role; it is part of that planning to identify the uncertainties and to have contingency plans available to deal with the likeliest alternatives. The most important feature of planning is flexibility, to ensure that an organisation doesn't adhere to rigid strategies drawn up in preparation for contexts which are no longer valid.

The need for flexibility is not the same as informality; the formality of the plan and the planning process is independent of the degree of flexibility or rigidity in the strategic options open to the organisation. Formality relates to the *nature* of the plan (is it written down and, if so, how is it constructed?) and to the *process* by which the plan is developed. The flexibility of the plan relates to its *management:* the way it is drawn up and used, and the way managers themselves relate to the plan.

Formality or informality – nature and process

The degree of formality appropriate to marketing planning is a function of the:

- size and diversity of the market
- size and complexity of the school.

These two dimensions can be visualised as a matrix, shown in Figure 3.1.

A large school with staff organised into a matrix of, say, year groups and subject teams, with a catchment area which includes urban and rural, affluent and poor, and ethnically diverse populations, would be located in the upper left cell of the matrix. A small primary school with four or five staff, drawing its pupils from a single housing estate would be located in the lower right cell.

In the first example the complexity of the school's organisation structure creates multiple loci of responsibility, more varied communication channels and the consequent involvement of varying groups of staff in decision-making. A hierarchical or one-dimensional departmental structure presents fewer loci of responsibility and fewer channels of communication. It also reduces the number of decision-making groups to which an individual may respond.

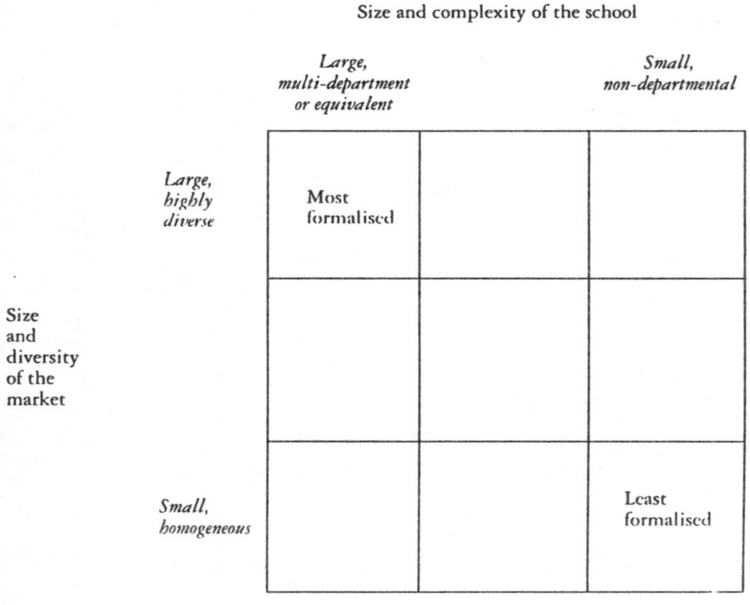

Size and complexity of the school

	Large, multi-department or equivalent		Small, non-departmental
Large, highly diverse	Most formalised		
Small, homogeneous			Least formalised

(Size and diversity of the market)

Figure 3.1 *Formality in marketing planning*

As the school reduces in size, the lines of communication shorten and the number of possible staff groupings, in either organisation structure, also reduces. For a small primary school, the division of staff into smaller groupings is almost impossible as the basic unit is so small. Furthermore, there are fewer people to inform and the methods of communicating information can be much simpler.

The market, where it is large and diverse, presents far more variables to be considered. The more dimensions that can be used to define the market, the greater the number of market segments (see Chapter 5) to be addressed in the market analysis and the marketing strategies. Thus, if the three dimensions in the example are defined as having only two values each (*either* urban *or* rural, affluent *or* poor, one ethnic group or another), this produces eight (2x2x2) possible variables to analyse the market by:

- urban, affluent, ethnic group A
- urban, affluent, ethnic group B
- urban, poor, ethnic group A
- urban, poor, ethnic group B
- rural, affluent, ethnic group A
- rural, affluent, ethnic group B
- rural, poor, ethnic group A
- rural, poor, ethnic group B

Clearly this is a rather simplistic categorisation but it does give some indication of the extent to which diversity of the market increases the complexity of the analysis, and the number of variables to be considered in determining future marketing strategies.

The nature of the plan

For a small, simply organised school, with a small, homogeneous market, the planning process can be very informal. The first stage of the exercise – market audit and evaluation – is easily done since the sources of data are few and the staff involved in the exercise can comprise all or most of the school's staff. The timescale of the exercise can be short, as little time is needed to collect the data or to analyse it. The number of alternative options open to the school will be limited and few people need to be informed of the outcomes. Thus the marketing plan can comprise little more than a short statement of agreed outcomes on two or three sheets of A4 paper. Much of the background analysis will lie in working documents and in the heads of the staff involved, who don't need to have summaries circulated, as they are familiar with the process by which outcomes were arrived at. It's only if external parties need to be informed that it may be necessary to explain how conclusions were drawn; even that need only be in summary form, as much of it will be self-evident.

Where the institution is large and complex, and the market diverse, the process of collecting and analysing data may well have been delegated to groups or individuals whose findings may well interact with the findings of others. Thus a group examining the choices of pupils at 16 (to stay on at school, go to a college of further education, start work, join a Youth Training programme ...) may find differences in behaviour between market groups along the dimensions outlined above (urban/rural, and so on). A second group examining population structures along these same dimensions may have identified changes in the sizes of the various sub-groups due to differential birth rates and/or migration.

A simple example will illustrate this. The children of affluent, urban white European parents have a high propensity to continue in full-time non-vocational education (this fact is evident in a variety of studies). A school with a catchment population which has a small proportion of such family groups but which has a substantial growth in this population sector (eg through urban redevelopment or the 'gentrification' of decaying housing stock) can predict that this may have a significant impact on sixth form size in the future. Gathering and analysing such data, through the internal and external marketing audits, drawing conclusions from each and identifying the implications, requires that the process be undertaken in a structured (formalised) way.

Similarly, the dissemination of the outcomes of the process is a far more substantial activity, with more people to be informed and more detailed information required to substantiate the strategies being pursued in view of their implications for individuals. There will also be more people taking responsibility for implementing the strategies and thus a need for coherent monitoring of performance to be built into the plan. Thus the form the plan must take will be a more detailed, structured and, therefore, larger document with much more precision about responsibilities, activities, timescales and intended outcomes.

Whether there is a formal planning process with a detailed planning document as an outcome, or an informal process with a summarising statement at its conclusion, the purpose is the same: to analyse the market, identify marketing objectives, devise appropriate marketing strategies, and to ensure that the marketing performance and its outcomes are monitored and the strategies reviewed.

At its least this could mean a primary school deciding to promote its playschool as a mechanism for encouraging parental involvement in the school with their pre-school children, as a response to evidence of the school attracting a declining proportion of children at age five. The numbers attending playgroup and of those progressing to reception classes are then monitored in subsequent years to assess the effectiveness of the strategy. At its most substantial, a school may decide to undertake a major restructuring of its organisation and curriculum provision, redesign its corporate image and change its name as part of a relaunch strategy to counter its long-term decline in market penetration and the perceptions held by the market of the school.

The process of planning

In either of these two cases the involvement of as many staff as is practicable is a key to the success of the planning exercise. Planning the marketing is a valuable activity to undertake as a staff development exercise, since it can also act as a vehicle for:

- raising staff awareness of marketing and its implications for schools in a more market-oriented funding and governance environment;
- team-building, as it can bring together disparate groups of staff in a process which draws on the variety of skills and knowledge they possess and engages them in a joint exercise to explore the concerns, values and aims of each.

The first stage of the planning process – the marketing audit and evaluation explained in Chapter 2 – is particularly valuable in forcing staff to ask who their clients are and what causes them to choose a particular school. It is a chastening experience to find that the bus route is more important than the glossy school prospectus in attracting pupils! It is too easy for staff in any organisation to become product or production centred in their thinking and behaviour. The process of exploring the market and the organisation's marketing activities can shift these perceptions far more effectively than exhortation can.

Although this is true for most types of organisation it may be particularly important in schools since the staff who work in them often have a degree of commitment to their role that is not present in, say, banking or insurance. This commitment is not something to be decried or discouraged in general, but it can cause teachers and their managers to have difficulty in understanding the concerns, values and aims of others outside the school. Addressing these issues, even indirectly, can give staff an appreciation of how the school ought to react in pursuit of its goals, and to question some received opinions about what should be done (particularly where inertia is cloaked in ideals).

Managing the marketing plan

The problem of planning is that the plan can take on a life of its own and generate an inflexible pattern of behaviour because that's what the plan says should happen. This is the complete opposite of what a plan should be about but reflects the inability of too many managers to distinguish between the plan as a framework of coherence for their actions, and the plan as a strait-jacket for avoiding reality!

A marketing plan contains three key elements which provide the framework of coherence (see Figure 3.2): the marketing audit ('Where are we now?'); setting objectives ('Where are we going?'); formulating strategies ('How do we get there?').

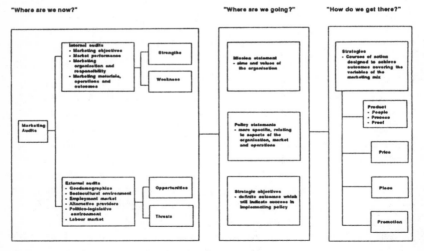

Figure 3.2 *The marketing plan*

The marketing audit

The first of these is, as far as possible, an objective appraisal of the school's marketing and its market environment and the relationship between the school and its market. In Chapter 2 the elements of this audit and the basic evaluation of the outcomes (a SWOT analysis) were examined. What the marketing audit does is to provide a starting point for the plan; subsequent events may affect objectives and strategies but shouldn't change the starting point.

Setting objectives

The objectives of the marketing plan derive from the school's mission statement; that sets the aims and values which give a sense of direction to the institution. The establishment of objectives is made easier if policies relating to the various aspects of the school are developed to give greater focus and clarity to the mission statement. Objectives differ from aims in two respects:

- they are achievable within a given time frame;
- they are variable over time.

Aims should not change very often; a school set up to provide primary education for a given catchment area should not find itself constantly redefining its purpose. At most it may make minor alterations to its mission every few years. However, its objectives for the next three years are not fixed so permanently; they might need to be altered if some unpredictable event occurs (for example, the building of a new housing estate) or if it becomes clear that they are unachievable in the timescale originally set.

Whereas aims are about direction, objectives are about destinations. Having arrived at a particular destination a traveller needs to consider whether to stay or to move on to a further destination. Thus objectives can be achieved and new ones set – which may include simply maintaining the present situation.

This is one aspect of the flexibility of planning: the setting of achievable targets means that, over time, new objectives can be set to maintain the overall direction. Progress can also be measured if clearly articulated objectives exist; just as travellers on a car journey from one town to the next can measure the likelihood of arriving at the destination by a certain time, so marketing objectives enable waymarkers (operational targets) to be set which enable performance to be evaluated on the way. If it is clear that objectives will not be achieved, alternative plans can be used, either to stimulate demand or to prepare for a level of demand below target.

Formulating strategy

In the same way that objectives can facilitate flexibility, the strategies being pursued to achieve those objectives should not be set in stone. They should be subject to review and their effectiveness judged in relation to the objectives set. It then becomes possible to ask the question: will the objectives be achieved? If the answer is no, the options open are to:

- revise the objectives and prepare for a different outcome than originally intended;
- revise the strategies to enable objectives to be achieved and identify the resource implications of the revised strategies.

(Of course, both options are possible, a revised set of strategies to achieve revised objectives.)

The plan enables such revision to occur because objectives exist, and the relationship between them, the strategies and the outcomes of those strategies has been defined. Monitoring these outcomes allows deviations from the planned outcomes to be identified and positive responses to occur. The alternative is for response to be no more than reaction to events outside the control of managers, and a permanent state of uncertainty (or crisis?) pervading the school. It is the way that the planning process and its implementation are managed which ensures that flexibility exists. However, it is flexibility within a framework which ensures coherence in the marketing strategies pursued and which ensures that innovation and motivation are channelled into a purpose, rather than being allowed to operate in an incoherent and unconstructive way.

Market analysis: aids to planning your marketing

If planning your marketing can provide a framework for marketing activity while allowing flexibility in marketing operations, it must be based on a thorough analysis of the market. The marketing audit provides a basis for such an analysis and enables the setting of objectives by establishing what is possible. The audit of the school's own marketing activity and market positioning (evaluated as its strengths and weaknesses) and of the school's environment (evaluated as its opportunities and threats) enable realistic objectives to be arrived at. The combination of strengths and weaknesses, opportunities and threats can indicate those outcomes which are possible (and probable) and those which are impossible (or improbable). It also indicates the likely strategies (or areas for formulating strategy) to enable the objectives to be achieved.

A school which has a strong reputation for sport but is faced with the threat of losing part of its playing fields to help fund new buildings could easily identify, as an objective, the need to convince the market that its sporting success is being maintained or improved. Equally, a school which knows itself to be weak in providing extra-curricular activities (clubs, teams, and so on) may see the reorganisation of the youth and community service as an opportunity to overcome this deficiency and set an objective of establishing youth provision using its resources, for its pupils, outside school hours.

Both these examples are simple but they illustrate the value of the SWOT analysis in identifying objectives and formulating strategy from an evaluation of the marketing audit. A variety of other more sophisticated techniques can be employed to assist in this process. Some rely on the cross-referencing of the organisation or its provision (products) with the market in a matrix. Three of these are outlined below; their inherent simplification should not be overlooked but seen as a mechanism for making sense of the complexities of reality. By forcing decisions about the meaning of the data collected, they indicate the possible range or nature of the objectives available to the school and the nature of the strategies needed to achieve them.

The Ansoff Matrix

Ansoff (*Corporate Strategy*, Penguin, 1986) divides the market and the product range (present provision) into two categories: 'new' or 'present'. The organisation starts, therefore, from a present product range in a present market. The options open to it are to:

- continue with existing products for its existing market;
- develop new products for its existing market;
- develop new markets for its existing product range;
- develop new products in new markets (See Figure 3.3)

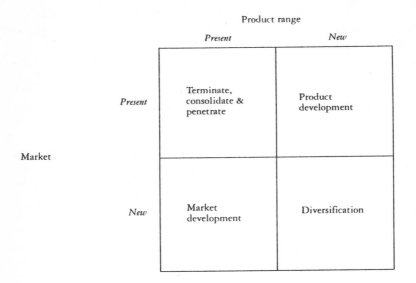

Figure 3.3 *The Ansoff Matrix*

While the first option involves no development of new products or markets, it doesn't simply amount to doing nothing. By terminating provision which is unsuccessful, product or market rationalisation is possible to consolidate the school's present position and, if possible, ensure a higher level of market penetration. Thus a school might decide that attempts to expand into a larger catchment area have not been successful and that increasing competition in that area makes it unlikely that it will be successful in the future. It therefore decides to cease recruiting in that area and instead focuses all its attention and resources in a smaller catchment area where it is the dominant school, with the objective of increasing recruitment from 80 per cent to 90 per cent of the potential market.

The second option would arise from an awareness that the level of market penetration is limited by the range of provision. Perhaps the school is seen as being successful in 'academic' provision but inadequate 'vocationally' and loses out to other providers amongst those parents and pupils keen to pursue vocational options. Thus 'product' (or curriculum) development is the most appropriate strategy to adopt.

The third option would be appropriate if the school can be seen to be offering a range of provision which would be attractive outside its existing market. This might be by attracting adults into GCSE or A-level classes; the product remains substantially unchanged, but the market is extended.

Option four would involve making changes to the product range as well; by offering adult education outside normal school hours, for example.

As a simple rule of thumb it could be argued that the risks associated with each of these strategies increase from option one to option four, as the development of the product range within an existing market enables the school to work within an environment which it knows well. The greater uncertainty associated with a new market, particularly when the product is also new makes outcomes much harder to predict.

The Ansoff Matrix indicates which strategies are possible and enables the schools to set objectives which relate to its two dimensions, according to the evaluation of both which the marketing audit helps to provide. The two approaches below help in that evaluation by identifying how well the school is currently performing.

The Boston Consultancy Group (BCG) Matrix

One of the most widely cited (and imitated) analytical tools in management textbooks, the BCG Matrix also provides an explanation of how the position of the school on the matrix relates to efficiency and effectiveness of operations.

The two dimensions of this matrix are 'market share' and 'market growth', each divided into high or low respectively. This creates four options into which the school's provision can be allocated, allowing performance in the various market segments to be compared to the developments in the market itself. These four options, illustrated in Figure 3.4, are:

- high market share and growth (the 'stars');
- high market share but low market growth (the 'cash cows' or 'props');
- low market share but high market growth (the 'problem children');
- low market share and growth (the 'dogs'). (See Figure 3.4).

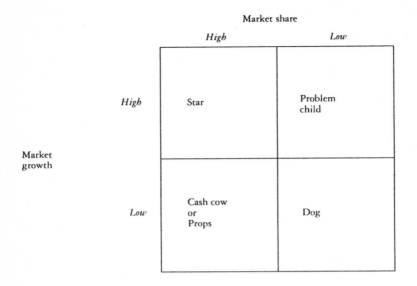

Figure 3.4 *The Boston Consulting Group Matrix*

The star may be a school in an area with a lot of housing development which is attracting younger families, and successful in recruiting most of the children in that catchment area. A dog would be a school in an area with substantial migration away from the area, which is in any case poor at recruiting from that area. The problem child fails to recruit in the first area, the cash cow attracts most of the children in the second.

Of more value is the use of the matrix to analyse performance in market segments. These can be parts of the market divided by geography, by social class or by any other relevant category (see Chapter 5 for more detail on market segmentation). A school may have a catchment area which includes large Victorian houses divided into flats traditionally occupied by newly arrived immigrant families. As they have assimilated and dispersed, new groups have arrived. Thus this has been an area where there has been significant market growth and the school has traditionally recruited successfully (a star).

However, changes in housing and immigration law and the expansion of local higher education have led to the housing being switched to student lets and reconversion to single occupation for higher-income families with older children. For a primary school, this changes the market from a high-growth to a low-growth or negative-growth market. The star becomes a cash cow.

The logic of the classification derives from a profit-making environment: stars generate profits and merit investment but cash cows should be milked for profit without substantial investment. Problem children will be low earners but merit marketing effort to turn them into stars, while dogs will be non-profit-making and should be put down!

In a non-profit-making environment the analysis is more complex; the model can help predict the effectiveness of marketing effort and schools must judge the validity of targeting marketing effort at the market by reference to their mission. A star is likely to be attractive to other providers and will need a level of marketing effort to maintain position, while a cash cow is less likely to attract competitors and should therefore require comparatively less effort to maintain position. Problem child areas should be evaluated to decide how appropriate it is to be in that market. If the school *should* be in there, it must be aware that a considerably larger effort will be required to increase market share (or even just maintain it) compared to those areas where the school is dominant.

The dog presents the greatest problem area for decision-making: should the school be in a market which has low (or no) growth and in which it has a small share? If it should be there it must recognise that the level of marketing effort required to maintain (let alone increase) market share may be substantial. The reason for this and for the varying marketing requirement in other areas is the effect of the 'experience curve'. The longer a school is in that market and the larger its market share, the greater the knowledge the school has about its market and the market about its school. Thus the school should be effective in what it does, have a high reputation, and enjoy economies of scale in those markets where it is a dominant player. The larger the market and the larger the market share, the greater these advantages will tend to be. The returns on marketing investment (the effectiveness of marketing) will be highest for stars, lowest for dogs.

The amount of resource per pupil recruited should therefore be lowest where the return is likely to be lowest unless the school regards its failure to recruit in a dog market as failing in its mission. However, it must recognise that the resources devoted to recruiting in that market segment would produce a comparatively larger response in other segments.

The 3 × 3 Matrix

This analytical tool is an adaptation of one developed for the US General Electric Company by the McKinsey consultancy. A derivative of the BCG Matrix, it is based on a comparison between the organisation and its market. In the form presented here it can be used as a summation of the SWOT analysis, since the school's strengths and weaknesses can provide one dimension, its market opportunities and threats the other.

The School's advantages are its strengths minus its weaknesses; this will include physical features and its market position. A well-equipped, modern school with a good reputation for academic success but relatively inaccessible to residents of an area which is attracting a lot of inward migration may regard its advantages in other market sectors as being quite high, but for that part of its market it may be quite weak.

The market attractiveness is determined by the opportunities minus the threats; this will include not only growth or decline in numbers but other characteristics of the population and the environment which determine market behaviour. In the example above, the market in which the school is strong may be declining, with growth only occurring in the area where it is weak.

This model provides three possible location points on each dimension: high, medium or low. By identifying in which area of the matrix a market segment lies, it is possible to identify the appropriate strategy (see Figure 3.5).

The model was originally designed as a 'business screen' to enable senior managers of a very large company to screen its operations to identify the areas where investment appeared justified (A), where it should divest itself of business activities which were inappropriate (C) and where senior management attention should be focused (B). Its adaptation to a school context doesn't alter this approach. In area A delegation of decision-making should be appropriate as others should be competent to manage marketing activity in these market segments. Senior managers should be focusing primarily on area B: it is here that investment of time and money might be required to improve school advantages or complex and difficult markets addressed. In general,

School advantages

	High	Medium	Low
High	A	A	B
Medium	A	B	C
Low	B	C	C

Market attractiveness

A   This part of the matrix indicates a market segment has potential which the school should be able to exploit and merits an investment in marketing activity.

B: This is the most problematic as decisions need to be made about the long-term development requirements of this market segment. A far more detailed assessment may be required before further investment in marketing activity is committed.

C: This is a divestment area; the school has little reason to be active in this market and is unlikely to be very successful at exploiting it since the school has few strengths and many weaknesses, while the market presents more threats than opportunities.

Figure 3.5 *The 3 × 3 Matrix*

markets falling into area C should be avoided and left for those more able and willing to exploit them.

What kinds of marketing strategies?

One of the most effective arguments in favour of planning marketing is that it makes the process of developing strategies much easier. The analysis of what can and can't be done which is provided by the marketing audit, and the identification of the marketing objectives makes the range of possible strategies much clearer. A school which is little known outside a limited area and which has set as an objective the raising of awareness amongst a wider population and a consequent increase in recruitment has an easier task in deciding on strategy, than one which simply feels it ought to undertake some publicity because everybody else is!

The rest of this book is about marketing strategies: what kinds of strategies are possible, how to undertake them, and their particular value in different market situations. There are no easy solutions to deciding on the appropriate strategy to pursue; however having carried out a thorough audit of the market and set realistic objectives, the chances of selecting the appropriate strategy are considerably heightened. Certainly, it's the only way to know whether or not they have been successful.

Summary

Planning should be seen as a mechanism to aid flexibility, not as a constraint on management. Deciding on the degree of formality in the planning activity depends on the size and complexity of the school and its market. A plan can be a simple summary of decisions by the whole school (if it is small with a simple market) or it can be a more complex document detailing the conclusions of various groups in a large school with a diverse market.

Managing the planning process involves a coherent, staged approach to establishing the current market position, setting objectives and formulating strategies. The marketing audit provides the basic starting point ('Where are we now?'); the mission statement and the various institutional policies provide the guide to the future direction ('Where are we going?'); and, from this, particular strategies must be derived ('How do we get there?').

This process can be helped by using various analytical tools to aid the the marketing process: the Ansoff, BCG and 3 × 3 (business screen) matrices each enable the data from the market audit to be analysed and identify outline strategies in conjunction with the school's objectives.

PART II

UNDERSTANDING THE MARKET

In Part I the concept of strategic marketing was explained and the relationship between the school and its market explored. The value of a coherent approach to marketing through the mechanism of a marketing plan was emphasised and the techniques of analysis which contribute to the development of marketing objectives were explained.

In Part II the nature of the market will be explored in more detail. Chapter 4 is concerned with market behaviour and the factors influencing individual choices. The notions of 'wants' and 'needs' are developed and their relationship explored, as is the way in which educational provision can be presented as a set of 'benefits' which relate to those wants and needs.

Ways of segmenting the market and the value of targeting marketing at specific market segments are considered in Chapter 5. Chapter 6 considers the need for effective market intelligence, including 'DIY' approaches to market research, and the value of establishing records which are market oriented.

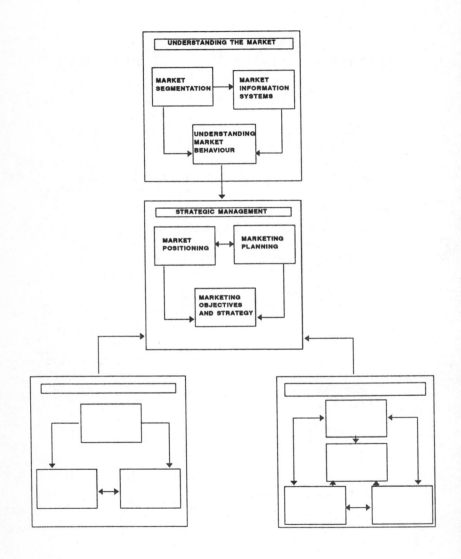

UNDERSTANDING THE MARKET

MARKET SEGMENTATION → MARKET INFORMATION SYSTEMS

UNDERSTANDING MARKET BEHAVIOUR

STRATEGIC MANAGEMENT

MARKET POSITIONING ←→ MARKETING PLANNING

MARKETING OBJECTIVES AND STRATEGY

Chapter 4

Understanding Market Behaviour

How rational is the market?

The guiding principle of a market economy is the notion of consumer sovereignty: through their buying behaviour, consumers dictate what is produced, how and when it is produced and at what cost. Underlying this is an assumption about the rationality of such behaviour. Consumers will judge the relative merits of the choices open to them and select those which enable them to maximise the benefits they enjoy.

For this to happen the market must enjoy access to as much information as possible about as many of the possible alternatives as are available. Thus freedom of choice depends on the twin supports of information and rationality. The absence of adequate information makes any choice, no matter how rational, limited – made without access to all the possible alternatives, or the fullest knowledge about items being chosen between.

Similarly, without a rational choice being made the option selected may not enable the maximum benefit to be achieved. One option, while superficially attractive, may preclude others being selected (through limited resources being available) which might supply more lasting or more necessary benefits.

Where state provision is available such problems were thought to be overcome by choice being removed from the individual to the state. Children were allocated to schools on a basis which was intended to ensure the maximisation of benefits to the *social group*. This approach has been subject to two criticisms: by the state arrogating decision-making to itself the freedom of individuals is reduced and the maximisation of benefits to them as individuals is not guaranteed; secondly, there is no guarantee that the benefits to the 'consumer' are being given emphasis, as opposed to the benefits to the bureaucracy responsible for making resource-allocation decisions.

A further criticism is also levelled at this model: that some individuals are more adept at manipulating the bureaucratic system than others. There is a tendency for more affluent and better-educated groups to benefit at the expense of the less affluent and less well educated.

The complete transfer of state-funded services into the marketplace would ensure the full force of the market (individual choice could operate) but would disenfranchise the worse-off at the expense of the better-off. One solution, involving the distribution of vouchers with a market value, has been proposed by many market enthusiasts but has a number of practical difficulties. The compromise between these two approaches has been contained in the reforms of education in the United Kingdom since 1988. Consumer sovereignty, through freedom to choose schools, backed by a market-led funding regime and a high degree of institutional autonomy makes market forces a very real presence.

This brings back the need for individual decisions in the market to be supported by adequate and accurate information, and for such decisions to be made rationally. The issue of information (as opposed to propaganda) will be considered later, in relation to promotional strategies; the issue of rationality will be considered below.

Wants or needs in decision-making?

Human behaviour is a response to a complex set of stimuli, some physiological, others psychological. Maslow suggested that human behaviour was a response to a hierarchy of needs, with the physiological needing to be satisfied before the social. Ultimately, self-actualisation needs can be satisfied. This approach has been very influential in marketing in developed economies as it provides a rationale for consumption behaviour which clearly fails to satisfy basic physical needs.

How far such needs are stimulated by innate drives and how far by learned drives is not directly relevant to a consideration of the rationality of such decisions. The principle of rationality is that individuals will allocate their personal resources to achieve the maximum benefit for themselves (to satisfy their needs). Given that there is a legal requirement for children to attend school and that there are few (but not necessarily no) monetary implications of choosing between schools, the major resource-allocation decision relates to the 'opportunity cost' of each school.

Opportunity cost is the next best alternative foregone; by going to one school pupils cannot be at another and thus lose the benefits attaching to attendance there. It can also involve a loss of free time if the travel time is greater, and a loss of certain freedoms according to the variations in ethos and disciplinary regimes between schools.

Counterposed against such opportunity costs are the perceived benefits which the schools appear to offer. These can include ethos, success in achieving particular educational outcomes (examination successes, and so on), proximity, continuity of friendships, and the like. If such decisions can be made by a process of rational comparison between alternatives then the market will ensure that individuals maximise their benefits. The assumption of a market-based system is that if each individual maximises her or his benefit, the social group maximises its benefits.

Benefits and needs

The benefits experienced by the market arise from the satisfaction of wants and needs; these two concepts can best be thought of as, respectively, the overt and covert dimensions of the same thing. Wants are the expression of an underlying need, the difference between the two being the level at which they occur and the intermediating effect of personality, attitudes and the social and economic environment. I may be hungry and needing food, but the food I want will reflect social and cultural conditioning and a host of other factors.

One important outcome of these intermediating factors is the balancing of needs and the willingness to defer gratification now for gratification later, which may bring greater satisfaction in the longer term. When I'm hungry I might want to eat anything but I will restrain that wish for immediate gratification while I cook something which will provide far greater gratification of need. Education tends to offer longer-term rather than immediate gratification; the longer one participates and the harder one works, the greater the promised future benefits. There is evidence to suggest that socialisation encourages some social groups to be willing to wait for delayed gratification and thus achieve greater benefits in the long term. The stratification of society is in large part a reflection of these different patterns of behaviour and is, in turn, further reinforced by them.

For the school manager, appreciating this distinction is important, since teachers by definition have been socialised to expect to wait for the benefits from a course of action, having themselves remained in education for five or more years beyond compulsory school-leaving age.

This can result in rational behaviour being too easily defined as accepting those values which we, as observers, hold. Marketing, on the other hand, is about understanding the values held by *others* and expressing the benefits the school can offer in ways which meet the needs of the individuals. It is rational behaviour for the individual to choose between options which best satisfy her or his perceived needs, however much that perception of need may differ from ours.

Identifying those benefits of education which satisfy the wants and needs of clients means looking at what the school can offer from the point of view of the clients. Adopting this market orientation, rather than production orientation, is difficult but necessary if the provider of education wants to communicate its benefits to the market.

To the provider, education consists of a variety of different teaching and learning strategies (the school curriculum) within a particular organisational framework and set of resources (the school). To the clients of that school (the pupils, their parents, the community) the school is essentially about benefits: will that school and its curriculum ensure that the clients' wants and needs are satisfied?

The benefits offered by the school to its various clients might include:

- a good attendance record and motivations to learning;
- a reputation for encouraging good behaviour in and out of school;
- efficient and effective resource utilization;
- a chance to study particular subjects;

- increased educational outcomes as measured by improved examination results;
- higher progression rates into employment or higher education.

To the school, *how* these benefits are provided is a major concern; to the market, *that* they are provided is the only concern. The market-oriented school needs to identify what benefits the market is seeking from the school and what benefits the market will expect in future. It must then organise itself in such a way that its provision ensures that those benefits are available, as far as its resources and its mission enable it to do so. Only then can it undertake effective promotional strategies.

There are also a variety of competitive pressures on the school from others which appear to offer the market the same or superior benefits. It is important that the school, in promoting the benefits it can offer, does not switch the emphasis from *what* benefits it can offer (a market-oriented approach) to *how* it will offer them (a production-oriented approach). While it is important to convince the market that benefits can be delivered, it is equally important not to get side-tracked into the detail of a school's operations as a counter to others' promotional strategies.

Benefits are the outcomes of the educational provision available; they are the satisfaction of market wants and needs and they must be presented in ways which relate to the market's perceptions and awareness of those wants and needs. It is through this approach that market behaviour can be influenced and rational choices occur, as individuals' decisions are made based on a comparison between what they want and what they will receive.

Identifying benefits

Expressing the educational experiences on offer as benefits is not easy – it involves the school in analysing the outcomes of the process rather than the process itself, and comparing these outcomes to the wants and needs of the market. These latter are the hardest to define and depend upon a clear analysis of the market; as was emphasised in Chapter 2, understanding the market is a necessary condition for effective marketing. (In Chapter 6, strategies for identifying market trends, behaviour and perceptions are examined and these can provide indicators of wants and needs.)

Identifying the outcomes of the educational process and expressing these as benefits is far easier, once the principle has been established. Most activities and procedures in a school are undertaken for a purpose; isolating that purpose from the process is the major prerequisite for identifying benefits (see Figure 4.1).

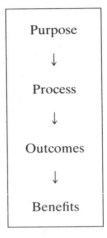

Figure 4.1 *Identifying benefits*

A further advantage of switching the emphasis from the process itself to the benefits for pupils and their parents is that the way in which the provision is described is more likely to be in language accessible to the market. Education, like most industries, has developed its own terminology which facilitates communication within the profession. However, specialist jargon such as acronyms also has the effect of excluding those who are not part of the system. By describing the education process in terms of the benefits to the market from its outcomes this barrier to communication can be removed.

Thus continuous assessment (*process*) enables pupils and others to know how they are progressing during a course of study (*outcome*). This in turn enables them to forecast their results more effectively and also to identify the consequences of putting more or less effort into their work (*benefits*). Offering Spanish as the main foreign language, rather than French (*process*), means that pupils will be be able to communicate in a language spoken far more widely than French (*outcome*), will have far more opportunity to use it – on holiday – and have a distinctive ability to offer in seeking employment or higher education (*benefits*).

This emphasis on benefits may seem like common sense, but it can all too easily be overlooked. A school with its own swimming pool has nothing to offer unless that swimming pool can be used for children to learn to swim and/or to practise life-saving. The benefits arising from having a swimming pool are what make it a feature to emphasise in promotion. A sophisticated laboratory offers no reason to choose a particular school unless pupils can benefit from it, through a greater level of knowledge about, skill in, or enthusiasm for, science. It is through the benefits *they* gain that a reason to choose the school exists.

Summary

The market has been introduced into the education system because it is believed to ensure that resources are allocated more efficiently and that individuals can maximise their benefits. This is based on assumptions about the rationality of individual behaviour and the availability of adequate information to aid decision-making.

The benefits sought by individuals are to satisfy their wants and underlying needs; schools must focus far more on these wants and needs to identify the benefits they can offer if they are to influence decision-making. This means adopting a market perspective and expressing the provision offered by the school in terms that reflect individuals' wants and needs rather than the *process* by which those benefits are derived. This is helped by considering the outcomes of the process and seeing how these outcomes might enable participants to benefit from the process.

Chapter 5

Segmenting the Market

Market segmentation : the concept explained

The whole market consists of individuals, each with his or her own patterns of behaviour, attitudes and personality. For the school, each pupil must be treated as an individual and given the care and attention he or she deserves. As a way of designing a marketing strategy however, individualised approaches are impossible. Standardised 'products' and promotion strategies must be used, for practical reasons. Market segmentation provides the school with a technique for matching the individual wants and needs of the market by using resources more economically than if it was regarded as a homogeneous whole.

The market can be likened to an orange: once the skin is peeled away it is revealed to be made up of various separate segments. The logic of market segmentation is that the individuals within a particular segment have behaviour patterns in response to particular stimuli, which separate them from others (who will behave differently) and which combine them together (because they behave similarly).

Anyone who has taken out a subscription to a specialist magazine will have experienced the effect of market segmentation in practice. Many magazine publishers sell their subscription lists to other organisations who regard such subscribers as being part of the market segment which they wish to target (a marketing strategy explained in more detail below). The opening of the subscription indicates that a particular behaviour pattern is likely to be present which is a feature of the market segment being targeted.

If the magazine were a photography journal it would obviously be of interest to camera suppliers or film processors: the products are likely to be of interest to camera enthusiasts. It might also be of interest to suppliers of wholly unrelated products who know that (one of) their market segment(s) consists of groups who have a greater-than-average tendency to be photography enthusiasts. What is important is not that they are camera enthusiasts, but that the underlying reasons for their enthusiasm cause them to behave in other ways which are important to an organisation.

Furthermore, the various market segments may require different products (or brands of product) to be offered, or the same products to be promoted differently according to their tastes and behaviours. Market segmentation enables the message which the organisation wishes to send, and the products its produces, to be tailored as closely as possible to the wants and needs of the individuals within each segment.

Classifying the market

In order for market segmentation to occur it is necessary to identify those features of the market which are relevant for market segmentation. Some of them may be physical (age, sex), some socioeconomic (social class, family status, employment status, housing type), and others behavioural (hobbies, shopping habits). What is important as a classification characteristic is determined by its value in distinguishing one pattern of behaviour from another. Thus, if a school finds that geographical location of families affects school choice – with 90 per cent of families in one area choosing a school, but only 25 per cent of families in another – it can hypothesise that school selection is related to geographical location. (It is worth noting that school selection is not necessarily *determined* by location; the determining factor could be bus routes. It is the *correlation* between the choice of school and location which makes it relevant to consider location as a classification feature for market segmentation.)

Within the 90 per cent in the first area it may be discovered that all tenants choose the school, comprising 70 per cent of families. Amongst owner-occupiers, therefore, only two-thirds choose the school. The most important market segment for the school (currently) is thus tenants in the first area. The marketing strategies for the school, if it wishes to increase participation in the second area, must be devised in such a way that the benefits being offered to that market segment coincide with those which are attractive to the first area which is already heavily committed to the school.

So far geographical location and housing occupancy have been used to illustrate market segmentation, but there are very many others, and they can be combined together in a number of ways to identify groups who exhibit common behaviour patterns. The principal classifiers are outlined below; what is important about them is that they are particular to the person rather than the school. Thus young people who prefer one subject to another (have different 'consumption' behaviour in relation to the school's 'products') are not a market segment by virtue of that choice. They may be a market segment if they have other characteristics in common which correlate to and appear to determine that option choice.

Age

Both pupils and their parents will be distinguishable by age; a school recruits particular age cohorts at different times, so that this year's three-year-olds are a segment of the total market of future potential pupils ready to start school at a particular time. It may also be the case that parents of different ages are influenced by different factors when it comes to decisions about schools, reflecting their memories and their own experience of school.

Sex

A single-sex school segments the total market and excludes about half the age cohort. A coeducational establishment may need to be aware of the factors that affect decisions by each sex, which may differ. Mothers and fathers might also react differently to marketing activity, making it important to distinguish between parents by sex as two discrete market segments.

Ethnicity and religion

For many schools, awareness of ethnicity as an important issue to be addressed has stemmed from a concern about equality of opportunity. Such concerns can equally be addressed through the application of market segmentation techniques, since the identification of particular market segments is a first step to understanding the wants and needs of such segments. Furthermore, in communities which are very diverse in their ethnic mix, it is important that the distinctions between market segments are based on market-led definitions and do not arise from Eurocentric views of the homogeneity of particular groups.

This is closely related to issues of religion and it is too easy to confuse the two. While behaviour patterns and attitudes among particular groups which are defined on ethnic grounds may derive from religious beliefs, it is important to distinguish those which are sociocultural traditions of a particular group and those which are religious traditions transcending particular ethnic groups.

Social class

The range of methodologies used for classifying social class (and of underlying concepts) makes this a far more complex but important characteristic. The most commonly used systems for classification in marketing (the Registrar-General's and JICNARS) are straightforward to understand, if simplistic, and are illustrated in Figure 5.1. Both rely on employment as an indicator of the classification to be used and are reasonably effective in predicting social and economic behaviour. Although it is possible to employ more complex models, the value of these lies in the relative ease of application and their widespread use in social and market research respectively. This enables available data from a range of sources to be used for analysing behaviour.

It is widely recognised that social class and educational participation and decision-making are closely interlinked. In many respects they present the classic 'chicken and egg' syndrome when trying to determine which might have caused which in the relationship between education and social class. For a particular school this problem is irrelevant to its marketing strategy; parents in classes I/II or AB are more likely than other social class groups to prefer (and be able to pay for) private schooling. As a general rule their children will perform better in exams at 16, will stay on in education after 16 and will most probably enter higher education.

Conversely, parents in class IV or D will almost exclusively rely on state schooling; their children generally perform least well in exams at 16, are far more likely to leave school then and receive little or no

JICNARS (Joint Industry Committee for National Readersip Surveys) 'Social Grading on the National Readership Survey'			
Social Grade	*Social Status*	*Occupation*	*% of adults over 15, 1986*
A	Upper middle class	High managerial, administrative or professional	2.7
B	Middle class	Intermediate managerial, administrative or professional	14.5
C1	Lower middle class	Supervisory or clerical, managerial, administrative or professional	22.7
C2	Skilled working class	Skilled manual workers	27.6
D	Working class	Semi-skilled and unskilled manual workers	17.6
E	Those at lowest level of subsistence	State pensioners or widows (no other earner), casual or lowest-grade workers	14.8

Registrar-General's classification of social class

Social class		*Example occupations*
I	Professional	Doctors, lawyers, chemists, clergy
II	Intermediate occupations	Most managerial and senior administrative posts (including teachers, nurses and MPs)
III	Skilled occupations:	
	(N) Non-manual	Typists, clerical workers, sales representatives
	(M) Manual	Cooks, railway guards, bricklayers, foremen/forewomen in engineering etc
IV	Partly-skilled occupations	Bar staff, bus conductors, canteen assistants, telephone operators
V	Unkilled occupations	Office cleaners, labourers

Figure 5.1 *Social class classification*

subsequent education or training. Knowing these facts, and responding to them in the marketing strategy to enable the school's aims and
objectives to be achieved, is the purpose of market segmentation.

Geography and housing type

Location can be a major factor influencing schooling decisions, and
one closely linked to housing type. Geodemographics (the study of
population geography) has had an important influence on market
segmentation, particularly through the ability to link census data
(which include location and housing type) with postcodes to enable
direct mail to be used to target particular households. An example of
such a system – ACORN – is illustrated in Figure 5.2.

Housing type includes the physical attributes of the property (age,
size, etc) and tenancy (owner-occupier, public or private sector
rented, etc). These factors in turn will relate to social class so that it is
possible to identify, from a particular location, not just how far a
family lives from the school but likely occupation(s), tenancy, and so
on. If these characteristics are influential in schooling decisions then
location can be a critical characteristic for segmenting the market and
one which subsumes a range of other characteristics.

Employment

The use of employment as a basis for defining social class can make
these two characteristics indivisible. However, if employment can also
be defined in relation to employer rather than occupation, it may be
important for other reasons. In those areas where a dominant
employer exists it may well be important to segment the market
accordingly. A school which has a high proportion of its pupils with
parents employed by a single large employer is vulnerable to changes
in that employer's market. A decision to reduce its workforce because
of market changes may mean that the school is directly affected. Pupils
may exhibit behaviour problems, and staying-on rates at 16 might
decline. The school should be aware of the size of such a market
segment and, where it is significant, be conscious of the potential
impact its employment decisions may have. The school can then
prepare contingency plans, or deliberately seek to widen the employment base of parents by actively recruiting from other areas to spread
the risks.

			1987 population		
		1987 pop	*%*	*Base %*	*Index*
	Acorn groups				
A	Agricultural areas	1870387	3.5	3.5	100
B	Modern family housing, higher incomes	9240962	17.1	17.1	100
C	Older housing of intermediate status	9622087	17.8	17.8	100
D	Older terraced housing	2309623	4.3	4.3	100
E	Council estates – category I	7046273	13.0	13.0	100
F	Council estates – category II	4844799	9.0	9.0	100
G	Council estates – category III	3867644	7.2	7.2	100
H	Mixed inner metropolitan areas	2080276	3.8	3.8	100
I	High status non-family areas	2268742	4.2	4.2	100
J	Affluent suburban housing	8577830	15.9	15.9	100
K	Better-off retirement areas	2064291	3.8	3.8	100
	Acorn types				
A1	Agricultural villages	1431922	2.6	2.6	100
A2	Areas of farms and smallholdings	438465	0.8	0.8	100
B3	Post-war functional private housing	2313416	4.3	4.3	100
B4	Modern private housing, young families	1870727	3.5	3.5	100
B5	Established private family housing	3206083	5.9	5.9	100
B6	New detached houses, young families	1511279	2.8	2.8	100
B7	Military bases	339457	0.6	0.6	100
C8	Mixed owner-occupied & council estates	1885816	3.5	3.5	100
C9	Small town centres & flats above shops	2211957	4.1	4.1	100
C10	Villages with non-farm employment	2571793	4.8	4.8	100
C11	Older private housing, skilled workers	2952521	5.5	5.5	100
D12	Unmodernised terraces, older people	1353182	2.5	2.5	100
D13	Older terraces, lower income families	748562	1.4	1.4	100
D14	Tenement flats lacking amenities	207879	0.4	0.4	100
E15	Council estates, well-off older workers	1868836	3.5	3.5	100
E16	Recent council estates	1487727	2.8	2.8	100
E17	Better council estates, younger workers	2661338	4.9	4.9	100
E18	Small council houses, often Scottish	1028372	1.9	1.9	100
F19	Low rise estates in industrial towns	2485780	4.6	4.6	100
F20	Inter-war council estates, older people	1586035	2.9	2.9	100
F21	Council housing, elderly people	772984	1.4	1.4	100
G22	New council estates in inner cities	1073155	2.0	2.0	100
G23	Overspill estates, higher unemployment	1646156	3.0	3.0	100
G24	Council estates with some overcrowding	821826	1.5	1.5	100
G25	Council estates with greatest hardship	326507	0.6	0.6	100
H26	Multi-occupied older housing	200858	0.4	0.4	100
H27	Cosmopolitan owner-occupied terraces	572936	1.1	1.1	100
H28	Multi-let housing in cosmopolitan areas	386503	0.7	0.7	100
H29	Better-off cosmopolitan areas	919979	1.7	1.7	100
I30	High status non-family areas	1138397	2.1	2.1	100
I31	Multi-let big old houses & flats	834208	1.5	1.5	100
I32	Furnished flats, mostly single people	296137	0.5	0.5	100
J33	Inter-war semis, white collar workers	3072990	5.7	5.7	100
J34	Spacious inter-war semis, big gardens	2684265	5.0	5.0	100
J35	Villages with wealthy older commuters	1582134	2.9	2.9	100
J36	Detached houses, exclusive suburbs	1238441	2.3	2.3	100
K37	Private houses, well-off older residents	1218680	2.3	2.3	100
K38	Private flats, older single people	845611	1.6	1.6	100
U39	Unclassified	293884	0.5	0.5	100
	Area Total	54086798	100.00	100.0	

Source: CACI Market Analysis, 59/62 High Holborn, London.

Figure 5.2 *ACORN profile of Great Britain*

Geodemographics

This technique for linking together location and behavioural traits makes it possible to identify people's likely market responses by reference to their address. The basic principle is to use census data to identify housing type and social class, cross-refer this to postcodes and to use these as the basis for identifying households with potential behaviour patterns.

The primary uses for such systems are for market research and direct mail; systems such as ACORN and Pinpoint (a similar classification system) are cost-effective ways of market segmentation for national and international companies. At a local level, schools can adapt such techniques to enable them to analyse their current market and map this against the total potential market. Knowing that the school is particularly effective in recruiting from particular geodemographic categories (such as newer estates of semi-detached housing) can cause a school to ask questions about the type of families this suggests are attracted by the school and either consider how it can widen its catchment to other groups or look for similar residential areas to direct its marketing towards.

Geodemographics is an example of the conflation of several market characteristics to produce particular categories; housing type is an indicator of a wider range of market features, such as social class and age, which are likely to be correlated with it.

Using market segmentation

A school may find that its market can be divided into segments, each of which might be defined by a number of the characteristics outlined above. Comparing the size of these segments to their presence within the total market gives an indication of the school's penetration of each segment.

For example, a school which is one of three in a town and which attracts 30 per cent of potential pupils finds, on analysing its market share by segment, that four main groups exist:

- more affluent (AB) owner-occupiers living in three main areas;
- middle-income (mainly C1 and some C2) owner-occupiers living on five estates;

- middle-income (mainly C2 and some C1) tenants and owner-occupiers living in older council-built properties on four estates;
- least affluent (DE) tenants living on one estate and in five tower blocks of council-owned property.

Each segment comprises 22 per cent, 38 per cent, 23 per cent and 17 per cent respectively of the total market, yet the school attracts half its pupils from the first group and 35 per cent and 15 per cent respectively from the second and third, with none from the fourth. Its location accounts in part for this, but the school has developed an image which has led it to be seen as highly academic and exclusive. This has made it attractive to more affluent and better-educated parents. It must now consider how its relatively selective intake from the total market squares with its mission and its commitment to equality of opportunity, particularly in relation to minority ethnic groups in the population who are predominantly to be found in the latter two groups.

In this way, market segmentation can break down market penetration data to give a greater level of detail in market analysis. (In this example the school's overall level of market penetration of 30 per cent is, in reality, 68 per cent, 28 per cent, 20 per cent and nil for the four segments respectively). It can also enable the school's mission and policies to be compared to actual performance to assess how well it is meeting its declared aims.

Targeting the market

Two main strategies can be adopted in developing a marketing strategy. The first is to use a shotgun approach, 'spraying' the school's marketing effort in the general direction of the market on the basis that it is bound to hit something. The alternative approach is the 'sniper's rifle', targeting market members as accurately as possibly.

The shotgun approach is widely used in mass-produced, low-value, widely used consumer products where marketing effort is aimed generally in the direction of major consumers (usually women) without much intentional discrimination between ages, social classes and so on. Very often advertising deliberately features models or actors who are not immediately identifiable as belonging to one particular market segment or, alternatively, a number are used to represent a wide variety of such segments.

Targeting is used where only a subset of the total market is likely or able to benefit from the good or service and when that group is identifiable in some way. Insurance companies target newly married couples and babyfood manufacturers target expectant and recent mothers because these market segments are clearly the ones most likely to purchase their products.

The advantage of targeting is that the same or a smaller level of marketing resources can be devoted to a smaller potential audience with a far greater likelihood of success:

- Products can be developed which are more appropriate to the wants and needs of the market.
- Benefits which are being sought by that market segment can be identified.
- Messages which express those benefits can be transmitted in a format and language understood by the market.
- Media to transmit those messages can be selected which more accurately convey them to the appropriate market segments(s)

Niche marketing

Ensuring that the products of the organisation are those wanted by the particular market segment(s) has been emphasised many times already. The more a school offers a specialist product to a particular market segment, the more it needs to be sure what the market really wants. This kind of 'niche' marketing can be very successful for any organisation which has decided that it would rather specialise.

In education, the concept of the 'magnet school' is simply the application of the niche marketing principle. A school which concentrates on languages, sciences, arts or vocational studies, is adopting a niche marketing strategy. For the minority of the market which wants such specialist provision it has a product offer which is more attractive than the mainstream provider. For those who don't want to specialise, which may well be a majority, the school is less attractive than its mainstream competitors.

The attraction of such a niche marketing strategy lies in its superior market positioning for that segment of the market which it is targeting. It may have a small market share but it may also attract pupils from a much larger geographical area, making the *total* market from which it is drawing considerably larger than the non-specialist institution, and its *niche* market as large as that enjoyed by others.

Clearly, such a strategy depends on a number of factors:

- There must be a large enough niche in the market to justify such a strategy, in relation to the minimum economic size to make it viable.
- It must be possible to identify the market segments which are being targeted and to reach them with appropriate promotional materials.
- There must be adequate transport facilities to enable a geographically larger market to participate if that is necessary.
- There must be adequate alternative provision to ensure that those market members not wanting the specialist provision are able to participate.

No school should embark on such a niche marketing strategy before it has gathered adequate data to demonstrate that demand justifies it, and that it is capable of responding appropriately through its curriculum offering.

Brand proliferation

For most schools a niche strategy would be inappropriate, but some form of targeting might still be appropriate simply because of the nature of its market. Recognising that a large proportion of the market has certain features in common and will be seeking a particular set of benefits from the school can make it worth refining its product(s) to meet their needs. This might be a consequence of a particularly high proportion of members of one social class, or ethnic or religious group, or family type, or any combination of these attributes. Identifying what those needs are, and responding to them, enables the school to target its provision more accurately.

Obvious strategies, such as ensuring appropriate religious or cultural needs are met, or providing post-school facilities for the children of employed parents, are about meeting the particular needs of the market. This targeting of provision may well give substance to other institutional policies as well, such as multiculturalism or equal opportunities. This demonstrates the extent to which marketing is as much about the institutional culture, its aims and values, as it is about advertising or public relations.

If a school is conscious of a diversity of market needs, some of which are not easily compatible, it may wish to offer a range of provision designed to appeal to these different groups. This is another approach to targeting. Instead of targeting one market segment alone and specialising in its provision, the school might want to target several market segments separately and to offer appropriate products to each. This strategy of 'brand proliferation' is an effective way of ensuring that a diverse market is satisfied.

A likely scenario would be a secondary school which needs to attract pupils from several primary schools and also to retain 16-year-olds and attract others from neighbouring 11–16 schools into its sixth form. The image of the institution and the range of provision it is going to offer will be different for the different intakes, and the establishment of a distinct sixth-form centre would be an appropriate response. The sixth-form centre becomes a separate 'brand' for the school – a packaging together of resources (teachers, laboratories, and so on) which are used in the main school as well. Their appearance as a separate brand, with some dedicated resources in support (a head of sixth, a sixth-form common room and the like), enables the market amongst 16-year-olds to be targeted more accurately.

Targeting benefits

Having isolated the particular product(s) to meet target market needs, the benefits deriving from the product(s) need to be identified. Once again it is worth reiterating a simple but important principle: the *benefits* are what attract the market, not the *product;* and the benefits will only be appreciated if they are communicated in a way that the market understands.

The assumption that the benefits of a particular provision are apparent, or that all sectors of the market will be attracted by the same benefits, must be avoided. The tendency to describe provision – rather than the benefits arising from particular activities – assumes that the market itself can easily identify the benefits. It makes more sense to present the benefits clearly. Furthermore, different benefits may arise from a particular aspect of provision, or a range of provision may ensure that a choice of benefits is available. The purpose of targeting is to present to each market segment the benefits being sought.

The simplest form of market segmentation is the distinction between parents and their children. A school which wishes to encourage parents to select it for their children and encourage the children to want to attend should consider the extent to which the benefits it can offer are perceived identically by the two groups. Parents may well have a longer-term view, being interested in options later in the child's school career and in examination successes and progression opportunities. For the child, especially in the first months or so, being able to stay with friends, to participate in sports and so on may feature more prominently. Although both segments may be looking for the same benefits overall (the child wanting examination success, the parent wanting friendship groups to remain intact) their priorities may well be very different.

The identification of these priorities and the targeting of segments to present the most appropriate benefits to them is a more effective form of marketing. Just the simple process of producing one brochure for parents and another for prospective pupils is target marketing.

Translating the school's activities and policies into benefits is often a challenge: all too often it is not immediately obvious why something is done. Alternatively, why it is done may be obvious, but the benefit accrues to the staff rather than the market. If the school starts from the principle that it exists to meet the needs of its market – the pupils, their parents, the community in which they live – it should be able to justify all its actions as offering benefits there. Some benefits will be direct, others indirect, supporting the school in its main purpose.

To many people in schools the idea of being able to justify everything they do by reference to the market is seen as unprofessional or demeaning. Yet it needn't be: professional standards can only be justified if they achieve the goals of the educational system, and must be defined in terms of the pupils, their families and the community in which they live – not for the comfort of staff. The comfort of staff is justified if it enables the school's goals to be achieved by ensuring staff motivation and morale and minimising turnover.

Policies on the curriculum (subject choices, learning styles, assessment, setting, homework, etc), on extra-curricular activities, on discipline and behaviour, should all be justifiable by reference to the needs of the market. If not, it is difficult to understand why they are being adopted. If needs are being met, it must then be possible to demonstrate the benefits which accrue to the market and it is these which should feature in the school's marketing.

Targeting messages

Expressing benefits in a form that the market understands is as important as identifying them in the first place. It is obvious that where a particular market segment speaks English as a second language, presenting the benefits in their first language is sensible. However, it should not be forgotten that the choice of vocabulary, the use of words rather than images, and the tone of a message can be as off-putting for some readers as if the text *were* written in a second language.

The message which a school wishes to communicate should be tailored to the market; all too often those who work in education complain that their message is not being received or understood. They lay the blame at the door of the recipient. Yet if others don't understand what your school is trying to do the fault is not theirs. Start from the perspective of those you wish to influence if the message is to be effective.

Communication depends on more than a message being transmitted: it must be received and understood. The more unconventional a school is from the point of view of the market, the harder it will be to get a message across clearly and accurately. Conversely, the more that a message appears conventional, the more it is likely to be understood as such. Recipients will look for clues to which they can relate and around which they can construct their own meanings. It is therefore important to start by identifying the various market segments so that it is possible to predict what different meanings they will give to the message.

A simple statement that 'pupils are expected to take responsibility for their own learning' can be intended to convey the encouragement of self-discipline and maturity; it can easily be interpreted as meaning 'pupils are allowed to do what they like'!

How the various market segments will understand such messages is crucial. A school which introduces a range of vocational studies for 14 to 16-year-olds may find that this appeals to those parents who would like their children to enter some form of skilled employment at 16. The greater opportunities and the advanced status they will have makes this an attractive product strategy. Conversely, for those parents committed to a more traditional academic education, with hopes of progression to higher education, the availability of vocational options may well present a negative image. Appreciating this, and setting out to present the benefits of the vocational option in such a way that it appeals to one group while emphasising the benefits still available to the other is the challenge that must be met.

Visual images can be more effective than words in conveying a message. The owl is an attractive symbol for schools, conveying wisdom and implying high standards. For some cultures, though, the owl is a stupid bird, conveying foolishness and ignorance! Understanding what interpretations will be put on your images by all the different market segments is as important as the choice of words.

Targeting media

Selecting the medium to target the market is common sense. Yet all too often this is ignored, and inappropriate media are used to communicate with the market.

Identifying particular market segments, setting objectives in relation to each, establishing the benefits they require, and presenting those benefits in a form they will respond to is wasted if no thought is put into the best way to reach them.

Any medium can be judged as effective for reaching a particular market segment by reference to two criteria:

- market penetration;
- market spread.

Market penetration indicates the extent to which a medium reaches every member of a market segment; market spread indicates how many market segments are covered by a medium. The higher the penetration and the lower the spread, the more effective a medium is for reaching a target market: maximum reach (members of that market segment receiving the message) and minimum waste (members of other market segments receiving the message).

The two criteria need to be considered separately as the conclusions reached about each can affect the choice of medium or the message

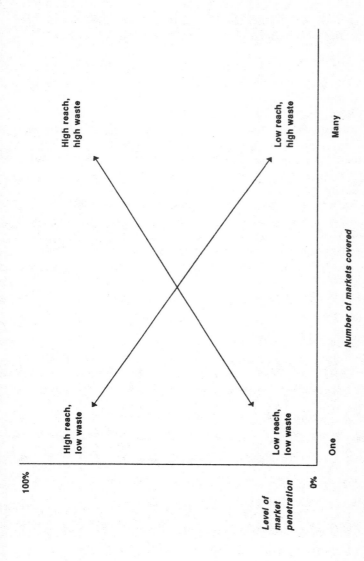

Figure 5.3 *Market penetration and spread*

A medium being used to target one market segment must be judged by how effectively it reaches members of the target market, and how many other people it reaches as well, on whom its message is wasted.

being transmitted (See Figure 5.3). A medium with low waste (few recipients outside the target market segment) allows for a message designed particularly for that segment, featuring only benefits they are interested in. One with high reach, ensures that most will receive the message.

A very tightly targeted message, designed specifically to appeal only to members of one particular market segment, would best be transmitted through a medium guaranteed to have a high level of penetration there, and little or no spread outside it (high reach, low waste). Where a standard message is being used, but this market segment is a high priority to be reached, a medium which has a high penetration of the market segment but also spreads across different market segments (high reach, high waste) is also viable.

Which media have these different properties? In general, direct mail (which may include using pupils as carriers) is the best medium for target marketing, while broadcasting (radio or TV) and posters are least effective. However, this is a generalisation and in Chapter 10 the properties of all the different media are examined and their suitability for targeting marketing effort considered.

Summary

A market is rarely made up of homogeneous groups; for a school there will always be at least two segments: potential pupils and their parents or guardians. Market segmentation is a technique for identifying the various components of a total market, using classifications based on individual characteristics.

This enables identification of the wants and needs of each segment and the benefits which can be offered. By targeting these market segments, messages and media appropriate to each can be transmitted, and products developed to provide appropriate benefits.

In extreme cases a school can focus on a single segment – a niche marketing strategy. More generally, schools can consider the advantages of brand proliferation to enable different segments to have a completely different product offer marketed at them.

Chapter 6

Information Systems

Knowing the market

Marketing has been defined, as 'anticipating, identifying and satisfying customer needs'. This implies a great deal of knowledge about the market. If empathy with the market is to be built up so that a market-oriented approach can be adopted, the attitudes, values and behaviour of the market must be understood.

How can the school get to know its market? In part it already does: the staff who work in the school have a lot in common with the community which the school serves; they are often part of it. They come into constant contact with the market, meeting pupils, parents, local employers and others through their normal work activity. The governing body or council contains representatives of that market and is able to contribute to an understanding of the market's perception in major strategic decisions.

All these informal contacts are as important (if not more so) than other, more sophisticated and formal techniques for gathering market knowledge. However, they may not be sufficient for a full picture of the market to be obtained. The impression which school staff have of market perceptions is not an objective assessment; too often it is the result of finding the information which is needed to justify decisions which reflect the provider perspective.

Governors or councillors, although elected by parents, are not fully representative of the market. For a start they only reflect the existing market, and not those whom the school failed to attract. In addition, they are not necessarily representative of the group they were elected by, since they are the ones willing to be elected. Although this does not prevent them from presenting a valid point of view, it should always be remembered that it is a partial one. Nevertheless, the knowledge which the staff and governors/councillors possess is a useful starting place, enabling school managers to ask:

- What *don't* we know?
- What do we *need* to know?

Finding out about the market presents a simple example of cost/benefit analysis. There is no possibility of acquiring total knowledge about the market, but a high level of knowledge is feasible – at a cost. Filling in some initial details can be done easily and cheaply, but as more information is required so the cost of collecting and analysing it increases, until a practical limit is reached. As more information is gathered, so the benefits to the school increase – until the extra costs of gathering information outweigh those benefits (see Figure 6.1).

In theory, these costs and benefits can be quantified and the optimum point established, where the marginal cost equals the marginal benefit. In practice, of course, this is very difficult, if not

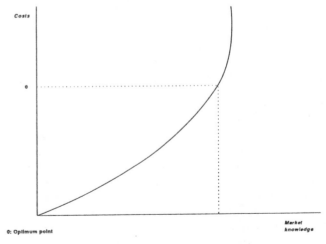

Figure 6.1 *Costs and benefits of market information*

impossible, to establish; the manager must make a practical judgement that no further expense (of money or time) can be justified. It is this judgement, like so many managerial decisions, which relies as much on experience and 'hunch' as on the quantification underlying the chart in Figure 6.1.

The definition of 'what we need to know' is the hardest to make. Things might be 'useful' to know, frequently 'interesting' to know, but in establishing an effective market information system it is important to identify real priorities. The information which is needed will be the information the system must generate, and which will incur costs. Figure 6.2 contains a list of the sort of market information required for determining marketing strategies. It is not meant to be comprehensive, nor is it listed in any particular order of importance, since importance is determined by the particular marketing decisions being made. However, it is indicative of the range of market information which could be collected.

Some of this information is quantitative, some qualitative; some is already gathered by the school or by others, some will have to be collected specially. Some will only be available if conventional market research techniques are used (such as surveys) but much of it will come through using a range of other approaches. It is this combination of types of data, collection and techniques which together comprise the market information system. The use of such a wide range of information types and sources enables effective marketing decision-making to occur.

Setting up a market information system

As has already been stressed, the starting point must be to identify what is already known about the market. Much of this will be a result of existing systems which were not set up as part of a market information system at all. Details about the current pupil population are held for administrative reasons; such information must be in a form which enables simple analysis to take place if it is to be of value. For example, a simple database of pupil's name, age, sex and address can reveal any changes which may have occurred in the past pattern of recruitment and the current pattern. Analysis of addresses is most easily done by using the postcode since this is designed to make it possible to sort

- Number of pupils, analysed by age and by family characteristics (location, family size, socioeconomic group, ethnicity, and so on) for the last five years.
- Similar data for other schools operating in the same catchment area.
- Similar data for the population in the catchment area (total potential market).
- Future trends in the population in the catchment area (growth or decline in numbers within the various categories outlined above and reasons for change).
- Economic, educational and social development projected for the catchment area.
- Quantity and effectiveness of marketing activity (eg expenditure on promotion, number of enquiries/applications/enrolments).
- Awareness of the school and attitudes towards it in the present and potential market.
- Awareness of other schools and attitudes towards them in the present and potential market.

Figure 6.2 *Market information*

addresses at various levels of detail. Only about six to ten home addresses share the same postcode; most organisations such as firms or schools have a unique one. The postcode consists of four elements:

- area (eg AAx xxx);
- sector (eg AAZ xxx);
- district (eg AAZ 4xx);
- address (eg AAZ 4BB).

A simple database can sort addresses against these different levels to make a geographical analysis possible.)

This kind of quantitative data, counting the existing market and analysing it by various classifications, is a useful starting point. After all, there is no point setting out to recruit more or different groups in the market without first establishing who is currently participating. Additional data which can be collected would include records of all enquiries, or all potential clients to whom information has been sent. A comparison of actual enrolments will show how effective the recruitment process has been (although not why).

Staff as an information resource

The first step in developing a more rigorous approach to marketing is the establishment of a system of recording clients in a format both comprehensive and easily accessible. A second step is to draw on the existing knowledge held by staff. The problem in most schools is less about knowing the market and more to do with making use of that knowledge. All too often valuable information, often qualitative, only becomes public by chance, as teachers, managers or administrative staff reveal something they had not thought of as useful.

A new housing estate is to be built; a large employer is closing down and relocating a lot of staff; another school has started a leaflet campaign or has been preparing a video; several parents have made positive or negative comments about another school. Insignificant facts (or even rumours) may be gathered together to provide a substantial body of information about the market. Although not quantifiable, such information can be of great value and should certainly not be dismissed. Gathering together is often the difficulty however, as much of it is ephemeral, and can easily be undervalued by staff. It is also likely to be equivocal in its meaning; unless they can appreciate its significance staff may be reluctant to mention it.

Techniques for gathering such market information include:

- brainstorming;
- focus groups or surveys amongst staff;
- open reporting.

Brainstorming

A useful place to start since it encourages staff to see that information is valued. Gathering small groups together (maximum nine, with between five and seven the optimum) and encouraging them to tell the group anything they have heard or know about the market can have a liberating effect. The fact that no evaluation is applied but the raw data are simply recorded encourages people to recall and express odd pieces of information far more freely. Subsequent questioning and evaluation can establish validity or relevance; it is an essential part of brainstorming that everything is accepted.

Focus groups and surveys

These more formal ways of gathering information are usually applied in the market, but are equally relevant when used internally. They are explained in the section below on market research. They enable free discussion (focus groups) or structured questioning (surveys) to take place in order to gather information.

Open reporting

A process for gathering market information as and when it becomes available. Staff are encouraged to record any snippets of market information which they have gathered, in a relatively structured way. The main problem is ensuring that a useful mechanism for recording and structuring the information exists, while avoiding bureaucratising the process to the extent that it is made 'user-unfriendly'. Above all, the information must be seen to be valued if staff are to be encouraged to contribute.

Once systems have been established to collect and analyse existing information, it becomes valid to set out to gather new information. The techniques used for gathering such information will vary according to its type; some are far more complex and expensive than others. No school should embark on a systematic programme of collecting new market information until it is sure it has exhausted all those sources already available to it.

Desk research

Desk research is an extension of the techniques already outlined; it involves drawing on existing data sources rather than creating new ones. However, up till now the sources have been internal to the school; desk research is essentially concerned with external sources. The data on the existing and past market are of little value unless contrasted with data on the total potential market. Knowing that 92 pupils from primary schools in the catchment area entered a secondary school is of little value unless the total number leaving those primary schools is known. If 630 left, the school is clearly performing very differently than if the total was 163. Sixty-six from one primary and 26 from six others is very different to 26 from one and 66 from the others. Putting the school's own market data into the context of the total market is the only way to make real sense of what is happening and has happened in the past.

Projecting forward into the future is equally important. Establishing how the market is likely to change enables longer term strategies to be developed. Given the ages of pupils which schools recruit, a primary school can predict demand three or four years ahead, and a secondary school about ten years. Where there is a choice of schools this only makes the *total* market certain, but the more information about the effect of location, social class, ethnicity, and the like on current demand, the more possible it becomes to predict future patterns.

During the 1980s and 1990s there have been some substantial fluctuations in the numbers entering and progressing through the school system. Although the average variation put the trough almost a third down from the peak, the variation in different market segments was significantly different.

Certain minority groups (particularly those originating from the Indian sub continent) did not exhibit the same fluctuations in birth rate. Amongst the majority population there were noticeable differences between higher and lower social class groups, with the former not showing the same decrease as the latter. There were also some variations between regions, with patterns of outward and inward migration having an effect, and between urban, suburban and rural populations.

Putting all these factors together, when pupil numbers were falling from a peak to a trough over a six-year period, some groups of schools found numbers halved while others enjoyed an increase in enrolment. Only by careful analysis of the demographics of the potential market and the school's actual market is it possible to make sense of these fluctuations and to project future participation.

The data needed to make this kind of analysis are available, although not always accessible. Education authorities often have their own research departments to collect and analyse such data. Planning and economic development departments of local government can also supply information, as can the Employment Department's local offices, the Training and Enterprise Councils (in England and Wales) or the Local Enterprise Companies (in Scotland).

The initial process of finding sources, gathering data, setting up databases and analysing the data is costly; once established, the maintenance cost is much lower. The value of the exercise lies in the ability to understand how the market is behaving and to be able to predict future behaviour. Without that, the school can only respond to the market as it directly affects it, and is thus unable to prepare itself to meet future demand.

As well as the quantitative data outlined above, desk research can also provide a variety of qualitative data. The regular reports and publications emanating from education authorities, central and local government, the press, various agencies and commercial operations, can all provide additional information to supplement locally gathered statistics. Qualitative information is often of value in providing a context for statistics, to explain why things are occurring or are likely to occur. Such information is often read by managers, but they are not always fully aware of its significance; making the connections with other information gives it its greatest value. The whole process of desk research is primarily about synthesis, bringing together a range of data type and sources so that the whole is greater than the sum of the parts. Only by a process of deliberate collection and analysis does this synthesis become possible.

Surveying the market

Market research is often thought to consist entirely of interviewers with clipboards stopping people in the street and asking questions about their purchasing habits. This form of survey-based research is only one aspect of market research: all the strategies outlined above for finding out about the market are also market research. The interviewer and the questionnaire are simply the most visible part of the process. The following sections will look at the principles and practice of surveying of the market, including:

- research methodology;
- sampling;
- questionnaire design;
- research analysis.

However, before considering using surveys to acquire market information it is important to exhaust all existing sources of information, and to be confident that information required is absolutely essential. The reasons for this are twofold: surveys are expensive, of time and materials, and require a knowledge of the methodology outlined below if they are to be reliable. The idea that a teacher or manager in a school can sit down one afternoon and design a research programme is as fallacious as the idea that a market researcher could walk into a school and be a competent teacher after half an hour's reading! This health warning is not meant lightly: market research requires a level of knowledge and skill which can't be acquired easily.

The following description of the process of market-research surveys is intended to provide an outline only; help and advice from professionals experienced in market or social research are essential if worthwhile research is to be undertaken.

The underlying principle of market research is that by undertaking a survey of a sample of the population the results can be extrapolated to the whole population. (In this context the population – or universe – is defined as that group of people or organisations about whom the researcher wishes to acquire information.) The assumption is that by asking questions, the information gained will give an accurate description of attitudes, beliefs and behaviour. Clearly this requires that the required information is known by the respondents, the questions understood and answered truthfully, the answers understood and interpreted accurately. Although this involves the application of scientific principles, the process is closer to an art than a science!

The sampling process is more scientific, depending on well-established statistical principles. There are a variety of ways of drawing a sample, and a range of different question styles which can be used to obtain information. Before either is considered, the first step is to determine the form which the research will take, since the face-to-face interview is only one of many techniques for surveying respondents. Each of the eight principal research designs outlined below could be subdivided into a number of variants; these descriptions are meant to give a general introduction to the most common approaches.

Personal interview

The face-to-face interview in the street, at home or in the workplace is the most commonly used form for market and social research and opinion polls. It relies on the use of interviewers trained to be neutral and to ask the questions only as set out on the interview schedule (as the questionnaire is called when not self-completed). It enables a number of variants to be used in the design of the survey which are otherwise not possible, including prompt cards and probes, some forms of quota and purposive sampling, and interviewer assessment of respondents such as physical attributes, sex, housing type and so on.

As a general rule of thumb, personal interviews are the most effective form of survey. One proviso, however, is interviewer bias: the interviewer, as intermediator between respondent and researcher, can alter the wording of questions or answers either inadvertently or otherwise. This is why training of interviewers is so important: They must be trained to follow the instructions on sample selection, interviewing and the recording of responses to minimise bias. (It is inevitable that a minimal level of bias will occur even in the best-designed research.)

There is one drawback to personal interviewing: cost. The need for each respondent to be individually contacted and interviewed (particularly if the more accurate random sampling designs are used) makes the survey an expensive exercise. In deciding on the appropriate research design a trade-off between effectiveness and efficiency is always going to be made. In general the decision whether or not to use personal interviews depends on balancing the importance of the sampling design, the need for interviewer control, and the value of the resulting information to the sponsoring organisaton.

Telephone interview

Some of the costs of the personal interview can be overcome by using telephone interviews. The interviewer can still keep control of the interview, and respondents can be selected by randomised systems (not fully random: non-telephone households are automatically excluded). There is a risk of higher rejection rates as it is easier to say no over the phone than to a personal visitor. It is also much harder to include questions which are anything more than simple recall since respondents cannot be shown any materials (prompts to help them with more complex questions). Nor is it possible for interviewers to include any information from personal assessment as they cannot see their respondents.

Telephone interviewing does have some advantages, however. It is much cheaper than personal interviewing, and can be much quicker. Telephone interviews can allow direct input of responses to computers (computer aided telephone interviewing or CATI) which cuts down costs further by obviating paper-based interview schedules (the computer can provide question prompts to the interviewer) and double-entry of responses.

A survey which asks 'Did you visit school A?' can easily be undertaken using telephone interviewing, but as soon as opinions are sought, weaknesses start to appear. As will be explained later, the design of questions relating to opinions or attitudes, often using rating scales, is undertaken more easily with face-to-face interviews or with self-completion questionnaires. Although they can be used over the telephone, there are limitations to do with simpler scales (three-point rather than five or seven) and addressing more straightforward issues. As with most research designs, positive and negative features have to be balanced in determining the optimum approach.

Self-completion questionnaire

Easily the lowest-cost option for gathering data from the market through the use of surveys, but also one of the most unreliable! The self-completion questionnaire can be distributed in a number of ways: to groups (such as pupils) in a controlled environment; to visitors to complete on entry or exit; to visitors to take away and send back; or sent out and returned by hand or post. The less control there is over the process, the more reliance there is on the respondent, the less reliable are the results and the lower the response rate is likely to be.

Over the last few years, self-completion questionnaires have been used widely as a way of gathering information from clients about their experiences of the education system. In colleges they have played a central part in curriculum monitoring and evaluation systems, involving students in providing feedback on their perceptions of the course and the college where they were enrolled. (An example of such a 'SPOC' (student perception of college) survey is shown in Figure 6.3.) These questionnaires have been administered in a controlled environment and have overcome a number of the problems of reliability and response rates. However, they can be criticised for superficiality: they are dealing with a very complex set of issues and, because of the inherent weaknesses of the self-completion questionnaire and the delicacy of the subject matter, they are only a partial success.

The weaknesses of questionnaires stem from the need to ensure that all questions are fully understood, with no mediator to probe respondents or encourage them to think the questions through. There is no possibility of ensuring that questions are presented in a fixed sequence to avoid prompting; for example, tests of recall without prompting ('Can you name any primary schools in the area?') cannot be followed by prompted recall tests ('Have you heard of any of the following primary schools?'). It is also difficult to prevent collaboration, unless the questionnaires are administered under exam-like controls, which is unlikely.

SURVEY OF FORMER STUDENTS

The staff of this college are keen to ensure that all courses are relevant and useful to the students involved. To help us achieve this, it would be very helpful to know of your present situation and how useful you found your recent course.

> PLEASE HELP US BY
> FILLING IN THIS FORM
> AND RETURNING IT IN
> THE ENVELOPE PROVIDED

DETAILS OF COURSE AND CLASS:
(To be completed by college)

....

....

NAME..

ADDRESS ....

....

....

POSTCODE: TEL:

INFORMATION SYSTEMS

1 **What are you doing now?**
(Please tick one box)

Please follow these
instructions carefully

In a full-time job	☐	*go to question 2*
In a part-time job	☐	*go to question 2*
On a full-time course of education/training	☐	*go to question 6*
On a Government Scheme (YTS, JTS etc.)	☐	*go to question 6*
Which one ?...		
Not working but looking for work	☐	*go to question 4*
At home or doing voluntary work	☐	*go to question 4*
Other – please give details		

....
.... *go to question 4*

2(a) Is what you learned on your course helping with your job?

It's very helpful ☐   It's not much help ☐

It's quite helpful ☐   It's no help at all ☐

(b) Please explain your answers to 2(a)

....
....
....
....

(c) Are there any areas of information or skills that were not
covered by the course that you now find would have been
helpful?

....
....
....

go to question 3

3(a) What is your job called? ....
(b) What is your employer's name and address? (We will only contact your
employer to ask how useful your college course has been for your present
job.)

Name of your supervisor/foreman/boss: ....

Company name: ....

Address: ....

....

Postcode: ....   Tel: ....

go to question 4

4   Are you receiving education or training now, either in a job
     or somewhere else?
     (Please tick one box)

              Yes   ☐   go to question 5

              No   ☐   go to question 7

5   What type of education/training are you receiving?
     (Please tick one box)

     Apprenticeship

     Course run at place of work   ☐

     Other training at place of work   ☐

     At college – 16 or 21 hour courses   ☐

     At college – day/part-time courses   ☐

     At college – block release/sandwich course   ☐

     At college – evening only   ☐

     Other – please give details   ☐

     ....

     ....

go to question 6

6(a) How long (in months) do you expect this education/training
      to last

      ....months

  (b) What are you studying?

      Name of course ....

  (c) Where are you studying?

      Name of institution/place of study ....

      ....

go to question 7

7 Read each statement in this section carefully.
Please tell us what you think by ticking one box for each statement.

	Very Good	Good	So-So	Below Standard	Bad	
The general appearance of the college	☐	☐	☐	☐	☐	
The general atmosphere in the college	☐	☐	☐	☐	☐	
The teaching on your course	☐	☐	☐	☐	☐	
The course content	☐	☐	☐	☐	☐	
The organisation of your course	☐	☐	☐	☐	☐	

	Very Good	Good	So-So	Below Standard	Bad	Received None
Careers help and advice you received	☐	☐	☐	☐	☐	☐
Personal help and support you received	☐	☐	☐	☐	☐	☐

If you would like to add anything about your college or your course please write it here:

....
....
....
....
....
....

Thank you for your help

IF YOU WOULD LIKE INFORMATION ABOUT ANY OTHER COURSES AT THIS COLLEGE PLEASE FILL IN THE DETAILS BELOW:

SUBJECT/SUBJECTS IN WHICH YOU ARE INTERESTED: ....
....

LEVEL: ....

DO YOU WANT TO STUDY PART-TIME ☐   FULL TIME ☐

DAY-TIME ☐   EVENING ☐

SPOC3 | PART OF THE SPOC/EPOC QUALITY MONITORING SYSTEM
The Responsive College Programme. FESC, Coombe Lodge, Blagdon, Bristol BS18 6RG | QUALITY ✓

Figure 6.3 *An example of a 'SPOC' survey*

Given all these negatives, is there any value in self-completion questionnaires? Clearly there is, as they are widely used. For simple questions where the respondents are easily identifiable and motivated to complete them, questionnaires present a very attractive research design. Where these conditions don't apply, the cost advantages start to disappear: a postal questionnaire would be regarded as successful if it achieved a 25 per cent return rate, so the production and despatch costs for four questionnaires must be borne for every response. Amongst existing pupils or their parents it is probable that considerably higher return rates could be expected, but for potential clients the result is far more likely to be at that sort of level. In deciding between, say, a postal questionnaire and a telephone interview, the expected return rate can be crucial for the decision-making.

Hall tests

This involves inviting respondents into a centre (traditionally a church hall, but specialist facilities and mobile units are increasingly used) where the respondent can see, use or taste a product, or view promotional materials to test their effectiveness. The opportunity to hall-test new products or advertising reduces the risks associated with them (in the 'fast-moving consumer goods' or FMCG market, a success rate of 25 per cent on new products is the norm) and enables alternative approaches to be devised.

Although hall-testing new products is not obviously viable for schools ('Would you like to try our new history lessons?'!) it is suitable for testing promotional materials. In one test of leaflets designed to attract 16-year-olds it was found that those least liked by adults were most attractive to young people; given that the design decision was being made by adults, their initial reaction would have been to reject the most effective design.

Hall tests must also involve some other form of research, either personal interviews, self-completion questionnaires or focus groups. They must therefore be considered in conjunction with the selected research design in determining the validity of the results and the costs of the exercise. Nevertheless, when major expenditure decisions are being made, or decisions which will have a significant effect on the long-term viability of a school (ie. the school's promotional materials) it makes sense to invest in a system for pre-testing.

Consumer panels

Again used widely for testing new products or promotional campaigns and also for auditing consumption or exposure to promotion, consumer panels enable 'longitudinal' research to be undertaken. Longitudinal research is research which occurs over a period of time, with the respondents recording behaviour or answering questionnaires periodically. It enables changes in attitude or behaviour over time to be recorded or the effects of external events to be assessed.

For a school, the consumer panel may be adapted as a technique by identifying a cohort of pupils for research into the effect of institutional changes over time, measured through the use of 'satisfaction surveys'. One criticism which can be levelled at consumer panels is that the inclusion of an individual may cause her or his behaviour attitudes to alter simply through inclusion (a 'Hawthorne effect'). This can be overcome by a process of rotating people on and off the panel so that there are always a number joining who may be less affected by their membership. Generally speaking, the less that panel members are expected to do, the less likely their membership is to affect them.

Audits

The audit is a counting exercise; it can be very simple or very sophisticated. The monthly Retail Price Index is based on a continual audit of prices of a range of typical products. The quantification of any event or situation which would provide useful market data may lend itself to auditing. If a school has an open day for prospective parents, or puts on a display at an exhibition, an audit of visitors will provide an indicator of the effectiveness of the event.

Simple head-counts are unproblematic and can easily be undertaken by unskilled personnel. More complex audits which include some qualitative assessment or categorisation of people (such as different age groups of visitors to an open day) clearly require a more sophisticated approach. The head-count is the minimum which any school should undertake for any event designed to attract potential clients to the institution, if it is to be able to justify the expenditure of money and time needed to mount it.

Observation

All too easily undervalued as a technique for assessing market behaviour or response to marketing activity, observation can be a valuable form of qualitative research. Observation includes the use of cameras to record behaviour for analysis by psychologists assessing how long consumers' eyes rest on new packaging or the route followed on entering supermarkets.

Such an approach is unlikely to be of great value to schools, but simple observation can be helpful in making decisions on particular marketing strategies. Should a particular location in a library or shop window be used for a school display? What times would be most appropriate for staffing such a display to maximise efficiency? Observation can help answer such questions by monitoring the number of potential clients at different locations and/or times, by periodic sample counts.

Focus groups

Terms like qualitative, motivation or depth research are often associated with focus groups. Unlike the other approaches to research design outlined above, focus groups are not designed to provide statistical data (how many people said they had heard of the school or visited the open day) but to enable a more detailed understanding of behaviour and attitudes to be established. The technique relies on gathering together a small group of people who are from, but not statistically representative of, the market. They will then be asked questions in an unstructured way (that is, not from an interview schedule) designed to encourage discussion at a level of analysis not normally possible with questionnaire-based systems.

The principle governing focus groups is that skilled and experienced group leaders can guide discussion without imposing their own views, assumptions or conclusions on the group. Analysis of the responses occurs through the group leaders' own impressions and through taping the session(s) and a rigorous evaluation of the discussions which occur. This is clearly labour-intensive and depends on the skill of the analysts and their ability to identify nuances of meaning.

The validity of this approach is often questioned; the fact that these groups of six have had a long and detailed discussion about products, promotion, prices and the like does not enable quantitative conclusions and extrapolations to be made. If a statistically valid sample has been asked a standard question ('Have you heard of school X?') 13 per cent of whom replied positively, and the population from which that sample is drawn is 100,000 people, then it is possible to state that approximately 13,000 people have heard of school X.

Such conclusions cannot be reached about a small and unrepresentative sample, replying to non-standardised questions. But it is equally difficult to explore all the processes and meanings which underpin the behaviour and attitudes of a population through quantitative surveys, unless hugely expensive and complex surveys are to be considered. Qualitative techniques can delve into these areas and uncover the mental connections which are not accessible through the quantitative route. Qualitative research is increasingly seen as a complementary technique, particularly at the development stage, when various designs (or products or promotion) can be presented and discussed and the market can have an impact on the provider before the finished product or promotional material is tested for real.

Given the qualifications which have already been made about undertaking research, it is nevertheless possible to adapt the focus group technique to enable a school to gain feedback from the market on its existing or proposed marketing strategies. The important principles are that:

- group members are chosen to be homogeneous, so that wide extremes of view are not likely to occur – this can inhibit discussion and produce argument instead;
- the group is formed for the purpose, is aware of the purpose and consents to participate in the exercise;
- the setting is designed to be comfortable, informal and non-threatening;
- the group leader is not, has not been and is not likely to be in a position of power or authority in relation to the participants;
- the issues to be explored are identified beforehand and a structure to the discussion is worked out to ensure that it addresses relevant topics and covers all the ground intended.

It should be stressed that this will not be as sophisticated or as detailed or complete an exercise as would be the case if it were professionally organised. However, it would enable a school to ensure that the general design and structure of, say, a school prospectus, met the needs of its intended market and had the intended impact on them.

Sampling

The principle underlying qualitative research is that a random sample drawn from a population will be representative of that population and that it is possible to calculate within certain limits the frequency with which certain responses given by the sample would occur within the population. It would require a textbook on statistics to go into all the details of sampling theory; however, it is possible to get an insight into the elements – and this is necessary if the different approaches to sampling outlined below are to be understood.

Randomness is the key to sampling theory; a sample is drawn randomly if each member of the population has an equal chance of being selected. This is more difficult than it might sound. Imagine a group of people visiting a school open evening. It has been decided to interview 10 per cent of the visitors to explore their impressions of the school. To this end, every tenth visitor is interviewed. If you are immediately behind the last person to be interviewed, what chance do you have of being interviewed yourself? The answer, clearly, is nil – so this is not a random sample (it is, in fact, a *systematic* sample).

Methods of drawing a random sample exist, but they usually rely on being able to identify each member of the population (by numbering names on an electoral register for example) and selecting names through systems for generating random numbers, such as computer programs or tables of random numbers. (Premium bond winners in the UK are found by matching bond numbers to numbers from electronic random number indicator equipment, known affectionately as ERNIE.) It is also necessary to have a comprehensive *sampling frame* (such as the electoral register or a school roll) from which the names can be identified. The sampling frame must contain all members of the population to be valid; a telephone book is a list of all telephone subscribers without ex-directory numbers, not of all telephone subscribers or all residents of a telephone book area. Similarly, an electoral register is a list of registered electors, not all adults in an area.

A properly constructed random sample is difficult to achieve and can be expensive, both in matching numbers to the sampling frame and in reaching a sample which will be distributed widely across the population. The larger the geographical spread, the higher the cost of personal interviews and, to a lesser extent, telephone interviews. It is for this reason that other sampling systems have been designed to

INFORMATION SYSTEMS

reduce the costs of sampling whilst retaining as many of the benefits
that a random sample has. The most important of these benefits is the
validity of the inference which can be drawn from the sample, to
predict for the whole population.

This validity depends in part on the way in which the sample has
been drawn, and in part on the size of the sample. The larger the
sample fraction (the sample as a proportion of the population), the
greater the *significance* of the results is likely to be and the smaller the
confidence limits which can be applied to the results. Significance
measures the level of certainty which can be applied to the result, and
is usually expressed as 95 per cent or 99 per cent (one in twenty or one
in a hundred certainty of a result lying outside certain limits). The
limits are amounts either side of the calculated figure within which the
actual population statistic is likely to lie. Thus it may be possible to say
'research suggests that we can be 95 per cent certain (ie. there is a 19
out of 20 chance) that 72 per cent of the population, plus or minus 3 per
cent (ie, 69 per cent-75 per cent), have heard of the school'. A bigger
sample could increase the significance of the result (to 99 per cent
certainty), or reduce the limits (to plus or minus 1.5 per cent), or both.

However, the size of a sample does not have to increase very much
above a certain size for these two statistics to be affected substantially.
A very small sample will have very little validity, but as it is increased
its validity increases exponentially, so that once a particular size has
been reached a few additional respondents can make the data far more
precise and reliable.

If these statistical data sound daunting, it emphasises the need to
ensure that a competent statistician is involved in sample selection and
analysis of the results. The following alternative approaches to sample
design enable samples to be drawn more easily. They don't prescribe
how large the sample should be or how significant individual results
will be. The answers to those problems lie in the details of statistical
sampling and analysis.

Systematic samples

If one in ten of a population is to be sampled, a random number
between zero and 11 (ie. one to ten) is selected, using tables or a
computer, and this gives the starting point on a sampling frame. If that
number were seven, the seventh, seventeenth, twenty-seventh (and so

on) person is selected. The first person is selected randomly, the rest are determined by that first selection.

This is an easy technique when people are grouped in any type of order (say, entering an exhibition) but it is liable to bias if there is a cycle in the population (a particular feature of the population is distributed cyclically) which could lead to that feature being excluded or over-represented. It can also present problems if people are able to identify the system being employed and deliberately arrange to be included or excluded.

Stratified samples

Where particular strata (similar to market segments) exist in the population which divide up the total into identifiable groups, it is possible to select a sample from each strata (using random or systematic methods) to ensure they are all included. The benefit of this is that a smaller total sample can be drawn to achieve the same accuracy as would be needed if the strata were not specifically identified, to ensure they are all included. This is particularly true if some strata are very small: it then becomes possible to select samples of disproportionate size and weight the results.

For example, an education authority has 1000 pupils a year progressing from primary to secondary education and wishes to identify the factors influencing the choice of school. It knows that 100 pupils live in outlying rural areas, whilst 900 live in the urban area where the schools are based. It can sample 50 per cent of the rural strata but only 20 per cent of the urban strata (50 and 180 pupils, respectively). The results from the urban pupils are then weighted by a factor of 2.5 to bring them into line with rural results.

Clearly, some detailed knowledge of the population is required to use stratified sampling but the value of it lies in the cost savings.

Cluster sampling

A cluster sample uses geographical distribution as the basis for sample selection. A group of the population which is clustered (located) together is used as the sample, either in total or by random or systematic sampling from the cluster. An estate of houses, an electoral ward or some other geographical feature is used to define the sample. It is particularly common when a national or regional sample is required since the spread of the population would make the costs of selection and interviewing prohibitive. By selecting a ward or group of wards at random then selecting within the ward(s) at random, a sample is selected which has most of the features of truly random sample.

Of course some areas are very different from others and it may be necessary to ensure that different types of area are included in the sample. This can be achieved by *multi-stage sampling;* the population is stratified to group together wards (or whatever definition of clusters is being used) which have common features and then cluster samples are selected from the various strata. In a local population, cluster sampling would need to be combined with stratified sampling in a multi-stage process unless the population is homogeneous.

The advantage of cluster sampling is the much lower cost, particularly for personal interviews and postal surveys (since distribution might be done more easily and cheaply). Instead of sampling across a whole town, one estate is used to represent it, or even one road. Its weakness lies in the tendency to find particular population characteristics dependent on location. The element of randomness is reduced and the more localised the population the harder it will be to select a representative sample.

Purposive samples

Purposive samples abandon any attempt to select randomly: they are drawn from the population because they exhibit particular behaviour or physical characteristics which are of interest to the researcher. A school wanting to know the attitude of parents of pre-school children may simply set out to select such parents by looking for adults accompanied by young children. As such, a purposive sample has the least statistical validity but can be very economical.

One way of improving validity is to use a particular type of purposive sample, *a quota sample,* which selects respondents to fill quotas of particular categories of the population. A sample of mothers of pre-school children could identify quotas for particular social class, age and/or ethnicity groups. The researcher might be given a quota of 10 AB Asian mothers, aged 25 to 30, because 5 per cent of the total population (all mothers of pre-school children) is known to consist of such women. In a sample size of 200, a 5 per cent quota would require ten respondents to fit these characteristics, and the researcher would set out to find ten such women.

The quota sample is the least-cost method of sampling and enables results to be obtained which are reliable enough to base decisions on. It has weaknesses: it is open to bias in respondent selection and can easily exclude members of the population because of the researcher's method for selecting the sample. However, its great strength is to guarantee that all major characteristics of the population are included at the lowest cost.

Questionnaire design

A questionnaire (the word will be used to cover interview schedules as well) contains two groups of questions:

- those designed to classify the respondents;
- those designed to identify respondents' attitudes and behaviour.

Respondent classification questions are used to identify the key characteristics of the respondents – age, social class, location and so on. All those areas which are believed to be significant in determining respondents' responses to other questions will be covered. Do older people have different attitudes to younger people? Do ABs use different school-selection criteria to DEs? Where a quota sample is being used they will appear at the beginning of a questionnaire to enable non-quota respondents to be eliminated immediately. Otherwise they will often appear at the end, to round off the interview and leave respondents feeling that the interview or questionnaire wasn't too difficult.

Classification questions are always factual – they don't ask for opinions, attitudes or beliefs – and they will be answerable in objectively validatable ways. The other questions may also be answerable in the same way, but they may also be answerable in subjective and invalidatable ways – questions about attitudes or opinions for example. However, for all responses to be quantifiable, it must be possible to group different answers together to count them, and it is for this reason that various *scaling* questions are used, which enable subjective ratings to be expressed on standardised scales.

Scaling questions are one form of *closed* questions, questions for which a fixed set of responses is available for respondents to select from. *Open* questions do not offer a set of responses: respondents determine their own answers which they or the interviewer enter on the questionnaire, and these will subsequently be *post-coded* to fit them into a particular answer set. Closed questions are *pre-coded*, as the answers available have already been established and the responses will be selected from the list, or will be fitted into them by the interviewer. Figure 6.4 shows two different ways of phrasing a question about age using open and closed questions. (The codes are used for data entry into computer-based analysis packages and help to reduce entry error.)

Closed:	Can you tell me which of these age groups you are currently in? (Circle the code)	16–24	1
		25–34	2
		35–44	3
		45+	4
Open:	Can you tell me how old you will be at your next birthday?		

Figure 6.4 *closed and open questions*

Open questions tend to be used in two ways: to identify answers in a *test survey*, in order to produce a set of standardised answers, or to enable respondents to express opinions about issues which they feel a self-completion questionnaire has not adequately covered. (They are rarely used in this latter case with interviewer-controlled surveys.) Some closed questions will allow additional answers to be written in but these should be rare, since a good questionnaire which has been tested should not have missed a substantial set of alternative answers.

The form of open question used in Figure 6.4 will often be used when an interviewer has a set of pre-coded answers, but is responsible for allocating responses to the appropriate age group. In self-completion questionnaires this sort of question will be used to minimise respondent error, as sometimes they find the closed question which involves selecting an age group difficult to answer. Nevertheless, closed questions are preferable (particularly with age and income questions and other 'sensitive' topics) as respondents are able to avoid being too particular in their answer.

Scaling questions, designed to test the strength or relative value of opinions, attitudes, beliefs and other subjective phenomena are designed to convert what is an essentially qualitative phenomenon into something quantitative. The most commonly used scales are *Likert scales* and *semantic differential scales*. Both of these are bi-polar; that is, they attempt to measure the strength of the subject matter being investigated by reference to extremes which are opposites of each other, with subdivisions between the two extremes to indicate the degree to which the respondent is drawn to one extreme or the other.

Likert scale
'I would prefer to send my child to a school which enforced a strict uniform code':

Strongly agree	Agree	Uncertain/ don't know	Disagree	Strongly Disagree
+2	+1	0	−1	−2

Semantic differential scale:
'I think strict uniform codes at schools are':

Fair	2	1	0	1	2	Unfair
Good idea	2	1	0	1	2	Bad idea
Autocratic	2	1	0	1	2	Democratic

Figure 6.5 *Bi-polar scales*

In Figure 6.5, examples of these bi-polar scales illustrate their particular characteristics. Likert scales contain a statement for which there is a set of *qualifiers*, ranging from highly positive to highly negative. The most commonly used qualifiers are 'agree/disagree', but any pair of opposites of a similar nature is appropriate. Equally three-, five- (as in Figure 6.5) or seven-point scales can be used, although the latter can lead to the extremes being avoided, while three-point scales may not measure sensitively enough. A central, neutral or 'don't know' option is essential, as this is as valid an answer as any other.

Semantic differential scales measure the various dimensions of a particular issue, and are therefore more sensitive to the complexities of attitudes, and so on. Thus it is possible for superficially conflicting views to be held simultaneously: in the example respondents may feel that strict uniform codes are 'autocratic' but nevertheless 'a good idea', either because they prefer autocracy, or because they have real conflicts in their attitudes which cause them to dislike the principle but endorse the practice (or vice versa).

Clearly, such question designs enable fairly sophisticated analyses to be made of respondents' attitudes and beliefs, and make comparisons and quantification possible. There are doubts about the meanings each respondent places on the answers given; some personality types are more likely to go to extremes, others to the centre. Whether this reflects true differences of emphasis or differences in expressing themselves is impossible to say.

Less sophisticated, but useful, techniques for identifying these qualitative phenomena are *rank order* and *forced choice* scales. Rank order questions simply require respondents to indicate order of preference for a list of alternatives. Forced choice questions present pairs or trios of alternatives; respondents are required to choose only one. Varying combinations of the range of alternatives makes it possible to establish an order for each one, in the same way as rank order questions, but enabling more complex sets of alternatives to be included. A simple rank order question becomes almost impossible to complete when the complexity of the choices reaches those shown in the forced choice example in Figure 6.6.

Selecting question types, writing, testing and rewriting questions and putting together the complete questionnaire are all lengthy and complex tasks. Ensuring that questions are understood, follow a logical order, and can be completed easily is the essence of question- naire design. All too often the novice at questionnaire design attempts to produce complex questions which are difficult to understand and sometimes impossible to answer. Consider this question: 'If you applied to more than one school, which schools other than this one did you apply to?' This is, in fact, three questions merged into one. The first question is 'Did you apply to any schools other than this one?' Only those replying yes to this question would then be passed on to the next two questions: 'How many schools other than this one did you apply to?' and 'Which of the schools in this list did you apply to?' All three are closed questions.

Rank order:

Here is a list of schools; please indicate your first preference of school by writing 1 beside it, write 2 beside your second choice, and so on against all those schools you wish to be considered for, in descending order.

School A ☐

School B ☐

School C ☐

School D ☐

School E ☐

School F ☐

School G ☐

Indicate your order of preference by writing 1,2,3 etc against the appropriate schools.

Forced choice

For each pair of statements indicate with a cross (X) the one in each pair you *most* agree with. Choose one, and only one, from each pair, however slight your preference.

1 (a) I prefer a school which streams pupils into classes at entry by ability. ☐

   (b) I prefer a school which has mixed-ability groups for all years. ☐

2 (a) I prefer a school which has mixed-ability groups for all years. ☐

   (b) I prefer a school which has mixed-ability groups for only the first year. ☐

3 (a) I prefer a school which streams into classes at entry by ability. ☐

   (b) I prefer a school which has mixed-ability groups for only the first year. ☐

Figure 6.6 *Rank order and forced choice scales*

A very simple rule applies when designing questionnaires: if it is possible to break a question down into two or more separate and simpler questions, it should be done!

Research analysis

Analysing the data gathered in surveys is the final stage in market research. A very simple questionnaire with only a few questions and a small sample is straightforward to analyse. Larger samples and questionnaires, again with simple questions, may be analysed on computer spreadsheets (Lotus 1-2-3, Logistix, and the like) but this is not ideal. The most appropriate way of analysing data is to use a programme written for that purpose. The most widely used is SPSS, but others are used commercially or for social and educational research purposes.

A good analysis programme will be user-friendly (easy to operate, with a clear instruction manual and usually menu-driven), will run on a personal computer (IBM PC compatible) or similar, and will at least produce:

- cross-tabulations (absolute and percentage);
- bar charts, pie charts and histograms;
- simple statistical calculations.

A table is a matrix, with response to one question on one dimension and to another question on the other. Cross-tabulation means analysing the response of one question by reference to the other. Percentage calculations can be done using responses to each question as the base, or by using total respondents. (For example, '10 per cent of respondents aged 25–30 said ...' or '10 per cent of all respondents said ...')

It is worth considering the vast number of cross-tabulations which are possible. Ten questions can be cross-tabulated in up to 45 different ways, and three different ways of calculating percentages are possible which, with the absolute data, gives 180 possible tables! The time needed for analysing the data should not be underestimated.

Data can be presented in *pictorial form* to aid understanding, and a good programme would enable this to be done without needing to transfer or re-enter data into another programme. Pictorial representation is often a useful method of impressing others with the results of the research and enabling decisions to be made which are based on the outcomes of the research. Clearly, this is the true measure of the value and effectiveness of research: decisions made as a result of it, or influenced by it.

It is often necessary, as outlined earlier, to specify the level of certainty which the data present. The ability to calculate certain statistical values and to undertake sophisticated analysis (such as factor analysis, regression analysis and the like) make the data far more valid than simple summation of responses. The managerial role means that school managers are increasingly making decisions based on complex data; it is important that they appreciate the extent to which statistical analyses can contribute to their understanding of the variables which determine market behaviour given the importance of market forces in the continued success of the school.

Summary

Adopting a market-oriented approach means knowing the market. The school manager has to consider how much market information is currently available and how much is needed. A market information system provides a school with a range of market data which can be analysed and synthesised to inform decision-making.

The simplest techniques for providing market information include collecting and storing standard information on clients in a format which allows simple analysis to be undertaken. Staff are a useful resource for gathering information and a range of other sources are easily accessible by desk research.

Only after these techniques have been exhausted should schools embark on market research. Quantitative and qualitative research is complex and resource-intensive; effective design of questionnaires, selection of samples and analysis of the data can provide masses of valuable information, but to be valid it must be done well – and that requires knowledge, experience and time.

PART III

GETTING THE PRODUCT RIGHT

One of the reasons that people working in the public sector find marketing so alienating is the jargon that goes with it. Much of this alienation is based on the use of the word 'product' to describe the output of a public service. For educationalists, the range of learning experiences which they offer and the institutional environment in which they operate is made to seem superficial and unimportant when described simply as the education product.

Yet there are good reasons for thinking of the services provided by schools as being products when viewing those schools from the perspective of the market, not least because it enables the understanding gained elsewhere about the relationship between the product and other elements of the marketing mix (price, place, promotion) to be transferred to an educational setting. The products of education are difficult to pin down yet the resources and organisational structures which provide them are very real. Those responsible for provision will inevitably become bound up in the detail of provision – 'production oriented'. The purpose of marketing is to switch attention from *how* the product is produced to *what* is being produced, the product itself, and to adopt the perspective of the market, to be 'market oriented'.

Chapter 7 examines the marketing concepts of the product in its 'core' and 'augmented' forms, and the roles of branding and brand differentiation. It also examines the notion of the 'product lifecycle' which provides a mechanism for understanding and managing the costs associated with development of new products. Chapter 8 is concerned with product management, identifying new product opportunities, designing and developing new products, and the key decision points which need to be observed in the process.

Chapter 9 is concerned with the product at a different level of magnitude, the strategic management of the 'product portfolio'. The manager's role in portfolio management is to ensure a balance across the product range so that new and old, growth and decline, are in some sort of equilibrium. Some of the techniques for market analysis (the Ansoff, BCG and Business Screen matrices) were introduced in Chapter 3. The way in which these can contribute to effective portfolio management and their contribution to decision-making will be reviewed.

Throughout Part III the concept of the 'products' of education will be examined and the impact on traditional approaches to curriculum and institutional management examined. Marketing is not an alternative to such managerial functions but rather presents a new paradigm, a new set of values and way of thinking about school management.

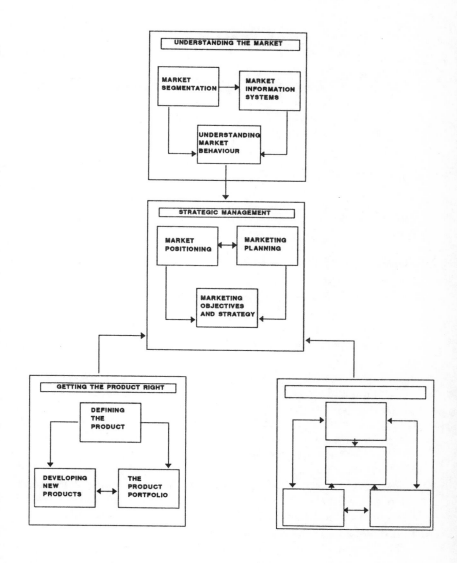

UNDERSTANDING THE MARKET

MARKET SEGMENTATION

MARKET INFORMATION SYSTEMS

UNDERSTANDING MARKET BEHAVIOUR

STRATEGIC MANAGEMENT

MARKET POSITIONING

MARKETING PLANNING

MARKETING OBJECTIVES AND STRATEGY

GETTING THE PRODUCT RIGHT

DEFINING THE PRODUCT

DEVELOPING NEW PRODUCTS

THE PRODUCT PORTFOLIO

Chapter 7

What is the Product of Education?

Knowledge or experience?

The product of a manufacturing process is easy to define. It sits at the end of a production line and can be seen and described, touched and used. When contrasted with education, the manufactured product should be unproblematic. Yet from a marketing point of view, the product as it is assembled is the beginning rather than the end. This makes the educational product even more complex a phenomenon to understand and manage.

The physical product which has been manufactured is described as the *core product;* it can be described in terms of its physical characteristics and is what most people would think of as the product. However, what most people actually buy is far more than the core product: their purchase decision is based on their perceptions of the *augmented product*. This augmented product is a consequence of the additional features which marketing adds to the core product – some of them physical additions (such as packaging) but many the consequence of promotion, pricing and distribution strategies.

The best way to picture the augmented product is as the outer layers of an onion (Figure 7.1). The core product lies at the heart of the onion and a series of layers surround it, augmenting the product and resulting in the final, purchased product.

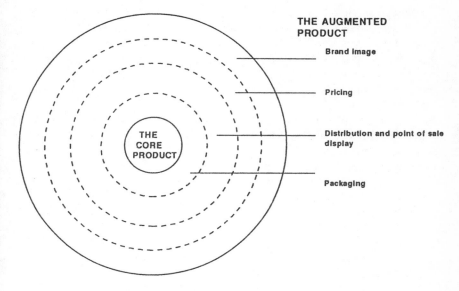

Figure 7.1 *The product 'onion'*

A good example of an augmented product is to be found every Easter, when a few grams of chocolate are packaged extravagantly, displayed prominently in every possible retail outlet (with the packaging providing its own point of sale display), priced at levels that all pockets can afford while appearing to offer substantial added value (over the bare chocolate) to justify the expense, and featuring strong brand names. Brands normally associated with snack bars or boxed chocolates are used to enhance the attraction, so that purchasers will be prepared to pay more than the cost of a box of chocolates for an augmented product which contains less chocolate.

For many people, the augmented product appears to be a 'con'. However, the extreme example of Easter eggs is used for illustration only; all products are augmented in some way by the process of marketing, however slight. It is important for school managers to appreciate the marketing significance of so much of what they do in augmenting their core product. Even when a consumer goes to a discount warehouse and buys an unbranded, unpackaged product at a very low price, that core product is nevertheless augmented. The benefit the consumer receives is not just the physical entity, but the satisfaction that comes from having made a bargain purchase. The absence of all the promotional extras – the packaging, display, sales effort and fancy sales environment – are seen to add value to the purchase by their *absence*. This paradox reflects the complexity of consumer behaviour and the need to understand that behaviour in terms of the benefits being offered even where such benefits are absences rather than presences.

For a school, the core and augmented product are far harder to define. The core product may be thought of as the knowledge and skills acquired by the pupil (this is the 'value added' definition) or it may be thought of as the learning experiences through which the knowledge and skills were acquired (the 'experiential' definition). The importance of distinguishing between these two definitions of the core product lies in understanding what is being marketed and how best to shape the product to meet market demand.

The two definitions are really cause and effect: experience is the cause of learning, the value added for the pupil is the effect. In the Easter egg example, is the product the chocolate or its flavour? The sensation of eating the Easter egg is one (and probably the final) benefit offered by the product. The *product* of education can therefore be defined as the learning experiences; the acquisition of knowledge and skills can be considered as part of the *benefits* resulting from that product. The design of the core product and the way it is augmented determines just how much benefit the market obtains, in the acquisition of knowledge and skills, and in a whole range of other ways.

Augmenting the core

The core product, as a set of learning experiences, may be seen as the *curriculum* which the school offers. At its narrowest, this can be defined as a list of subjects and the syllabus or learning outcomes of that list of subjects. This is essentially the approach adopted in the National Curriculum, where subjects and subject content (including the knowledge and skills to be acquired) are set out in some detail. Most educationalists would favour a broader definition of the curriculum, being as much about *how* learning occurs as subject matter.

The various approaches to learning, from the didactic to the resource-based, can be considered as part of the *range* of learning experiences offered by a school. Quite clearly, how a pupil learns is as important as what is learnt – and is reflexive, affecting what is learnt. The curriculum policies adopted by a school will be the most important demonstration of the values and goals contained within its mission (whether or not that mission has been formally expressed). This book is not concerned with the particular curriculum policies which should be adopted; it is for the school to make that decision.

What *is* relevant to marketing management (or any aspect of school management) is that there is some coherence to the school curriculum, using the wider definition. The curriculum strategy (what is being learnt, how it is learnt) is the school's core product; without some clear policy towards designing, developing, implementing monitoring and evaluating that core product, there is little point in developing strategies to augment the core.

The process of new product development is explored in more detail in Chapter 8. The design, development, monitoring and evaluation of the curriculum are the principal elements of that function. At this stage it is relevant only to stress how central to an effective marketing strategy is the need for some certainty about the core product. It is the centre of any system for assuring educational quality and is the only way that a school can be confident in its efforts to recruit pupils.

Augmenting this core product includes a similar range of strategies to those found in consumer marketing, although they may not appear that similar at first sight. Packaging, premium offers and branding are all possibilities, although their application may appear to be novel interpretations of the concepts. In fact, many of the developments in product augmentation have occurred in the commercial services sectors; insurance, banking and other financial services have had to learn how these marketing strategies can be applied to them. In many cases, they have found similar degrees of resistance to marketing among their staffs as schools will find. The difference is that many of the strategies are already being implemented in schools, being seen not as marketing but good curriculum management. A good pupil-centred approach to the curriculum is no different from a market-oriented approach to school management; the language changes, not the concepts.

Packaging

The idea of packaging education may sound surreal, given that education is about experiences rather than physical entities. Yet it is becoming more and more common to find services offered as a package. A solicitor will offer a fixed-price service as estate agent, mortgage broker and conveyancer; a bank offers a current account, deposit account, guaranteed overdraft facility, high-value cheque card and the full range of transaction services as an 'all in' account; an insurance company offers a comprehensive insurance cover for house, contents, credit cards, travel and illness in one policy. These are all examples of service packaging, and they have certain common features:

- They identify and offer a set of services which the market (or a market segment) wants.
- Individually, some of the services would either not be taken up in full, or would be more expensive if bought separately.
- The package contains options, either as choices between alternatives or as extras which can be selected or declined.
- There are economies of scale in offering the package which can be passed on to the market, either through meeting the higher volume of demand, or through the standardisation of service.

For a school, many of these features are already integrated into the programme, and the National Curriculum may well encourage further standardisation. The grouping together of subjects, the range of extra-curricular activities, the elements of the personal and social curriculum, the ethos of the institution and the structures used to reinforce that ethos (year tutors, houses, prefect systems) are all part of the package. What a marketing perspective emphasises is that these various features are part of the product, that they augment the core product, and that they should be presented to the market in terms of the benefits they offer.

The school should identify the 'package' it is offering and present it coherently, not as a set of disconnected elements. There is a clear synthesis in packaging the various components of the product; the whole becomes greater than its parts because the links are strengthened and given coherence. Learning, in all its different forms, is recognised, credited and valued, and the market can understand what is being offered and identify the benefits accruing from the range of activities and the environment which the school offers.

Premium offers

Premium offers are promotional strategies used by organisations to add value to their products; they include:

- price discounts;
- discount vouchers;
- self-liquidating premiums (items supplied in return for payment plus 'proofs of purchase'; they are designed to pay for themselves by charging items out at cost, hence self-liquidating);
- banded offers and bonus offers (two products banded together or extra product sold at standard, single-product, price);
- free or discounted samples;
- free gifts.

What all of these strategies have in common is that the benefits to consumers are enhanced relative to the cost (to them) of the benefits. It is not necessary to hold the price or lower it, more can be charged to the consumer but the product enhancement exceeds the extra cost. Thus a standard priced product may offer a self-liquidating premium (SLP); the consumers must buy products to obtain vouchers which can be used to buy the SLP which is charged out at less than normal retail price, or is a special line not normally available.

Of course, premiums can also be used to mask price rises or product reductions, and can be criticised as expensive alternatives to price reductions. The argument in favour of premium offers is that the benefits to the market exceed what would otherwise be available through price cuts. The basis for this is the argument of economies of scale; the extra volume of sales generated (or the maintenance of sales in the face of competitive pressure) enables cost savings which can be passed on. Simple price cuts would be met by competitive price cuts, there would be no volume increase and the long-term viability of the organisation would suffer, reducing consumer choice or, through lack of investment, reducing future improvements in quality or efficiency in production.

Whether or not these arguments are valid, where no price is charged to the consumer (as with state-funded schooling) there is no opportunity to cut prices. This is not to pretend there is no cost to the market, of course, because the market pays for education through taxes, through extra costs associated with schooling (from uniforms to school fetes), and because every activity exacts an opportunity cost. Premiums offer schools the chance to add to the benefits they offer through the packaged product; some of these may also be seen as revenue-raising opportunities for the school, but if their principal purpose is to enhance the product they must be approached from this viewpoint not as additions to the product range.

Some premiums are fairly simple: the issuing of school-branded exercise books and folders, and other materials to support learning. Some materials might be sold to pupils (folders, bags, sweatshirts) as SLPs; vouchers might be issued to enable such SLPs to be bought or to be used in other organisations (for discounts at theatres or concerts for example). In all these instances schools must clarify what they are legally obliged to provide, and what it is legally and morally valid for them to do. However, where they *must* supply materials or services, or believe they *ought to* supply them, they can still be used to support their promotion. Schlitz beer in the USA promoted their beer as sold in bottles 'washed with steam', to emphasise cleanliness at a time when bottled beer suffered from a poor hygiene reputation. The Schlitz promotion was successful, although all brewers used the same process. Marketing success does not necessarily come from being different, it can come from emphasising what is being done, no matter how common it is.

The school's product is not easily described; too often a description of a subject or an activity can obscure more than it clarifies, as technical language and unfamiliar experiences are communicated to pupils or their parents. If the product is right, and the school's principal offer is its product range, then the best way to express this is to provide a sample. It is becoming increasingly common for schools to offer sixth formers the chance to start their studies before the summer holiday, after the completion of their GCSE exams. This is sampling. The same approach can be used to attract pupils at 5 or 11 – it can also be used to attract parents or to demonstrate to other community members (part of the market) what the school has to offer.

Open days or evenings, which are meant to have a promotional purpose, can be sterile events if the main experience is one of empty classrooms, laboratories and workshops. If the purpose of a promotional event is to emphasise the benefits which a school can offer, those benefits are best promoted by experience; it also demonstrates the confidence the school has in the quality of its products.

The use of premium offers, or the recognition that standard procedures can be treated as premiums, should be seen as a way of augmenting the product through an increase in the value of the products on offer. Great care must be taken not to appear to be using premiums as a way of bribing pupils or their parents to visit or choose a school. Not only is such a strategy morally dubious, it will inevitably backfire since the impression it gives of the quality of the school is negative.

Pricing

Pricing is a marketing function, costing is an accounting function. Distinguishing between the two is important, particularly as schools are being encouraged to extend their product range beyond their statutory provision. Services such as post-school supervision, nursery classes and adult education classes may all be run as market-funded operations. Schools can also sell goods (stationery, food and refreshments, sweat-shirts, tee-shirts) to supplement their income.

The price charged for a product is itself a part of the product; it reflects on the product and creates an expectation of relative quality in comparison with other providers. A low-priced item can be 'cheap' – low quality as well as low cost. A high-priced item can be high value, and its quality commensurate.

Pricing a product involves considering the perceptions of the market and the need to recover costs. The market perceptions are derived from the experience of buying similar products, or the same product from alternative suppliers. It is essential, therefore, to explore the prices being charged elsewhere and to decide how the 'quality' of the products compare. It is also important to identify the extent to which recognisable price bands exist. These may relate to broad levels of product quality, with some products of similar quality all being in a range of prices. Setting a price midway between ranges can make it difficult for the market to determine what comparisons should be made, preventing them from judging the product and therefore inhibiting their selection of it.

Rounded prices (£1.50, £1.75) simplify change-giving and enable customers to recall prices easily. A price like £1.51 seems to imply that the supplier is being pedantic and small-minded in insisting on the extra penny. Conversely, prices like £1.99 or £1.49 have the effect of making prices appear lower than they are. £1.99 is 'one pound something', whereas two pounds is two pounds; the penny difference can be significant in encouraging purchase. If the price has to be over two pounds (say £2.02) demand may fall compared to £1.99; putting the price up to £2.15 may have no greater effect on demand, since the price barrier is two pounds and whether it is breached by two pence or 15 is immaterial.

The price should at least cover the total cost of an activity, unless it is regarded as being:

- socially or economically essential for the market to enable people to participate in publicly funded activity;
- a mechanism for attracting the market, to encourage participation in other activities (a *loss leader*);
- a marginal activity, only expected to recoup marginal cost.

Marginal cost is the additional cost of offering the product such as overtime for a caretaker, when hiring out facilities at weekends. However, if the school intends developing a service as a part of its core business it should expect to recoup not just marginal cost but an appropriate part of the school's overheads.

Once the costs have been determined, the marketing decisions about price can be taken. What are the prices of alternative products or suppliers? Are there price ranges in evidence? What implications do price levels have for quality? Are there obvious price ceilings? It is through judgements about these issues that prices are set which reflect on the product to augment it positively.

Branding

The brand emerged during the late nineteenth century as the major development in marketing; the switch of emphasis from the retailer to the manufacturer and the packaged product has now gone almost full circle, with retailers' own brands having as high a status as manufacturers' in some sectors. A brand is a way of differentiating one product from another; the greater the perceived similarity of products, the more important the brand in establishing the differences.

Some schools will clearly feel that they are different from others, or that the market perceives differences, which makes it less important for them to establish their corporate identity. However, many will be aware that to the market there is an apparent homogeneity about schools. Establishing that a school is different is not necessarily easy, but can best be done by focusing on a key feature rather than trying to emphasise a breadth of features which distinguish the school from others.

The emergence of City Technology Colleges (CTCs), grant maintained (GM) and 'Magnet' schools is largely based on this notion. The CTCs were originally meant to offer a science-based, technologically oriented curriculum, though that became less central, while GM schools would offer more parental control. Magnet schools are a variant on the CTC theme, being specialist in their curriculum provision and seen as centres of excellence, a strategy commonly used in the private sector.

This approach, the identification of a *unique selling proposition* (USP) provides the market with an easily remembered and recognised 'look' to which the whole range of provision can then be attached. A USP is usually expressed as a catchphrase or tag line that summarises the product(s) and the benefits they offer. The USP should also be tied closely to the brand being promoted; there is no value in everybody knowing the USP but not to which product or organisation it is attached.

The brand is both a *name* (which identifies a product or organisation) and an *image* (which adds to or detracts from the product or image). The image is far more resilient than the name; there are high schools and comprehensives around the country which are still known as the 'grammar' or the 'secondary modern'. The school must start with a clear idea of what its brand image is; this means being brutally frank and not pretending that the market behaves as we would like. It must then establish how it would like to appear in order to enhance its products. Closing the gap between these two points is the subject of Part IV; at this stage it is enough to emphasise the complexity of this task.

Assuming that the school is able to establish the image it wants, or is content with the image it has, it must ensure that this enhances its products in the eyes of the market (which is its purpose). It must also decide whether a single brand is adequate. The larger the school and the more diverse its market, the more value there may be in *brand proliferation* – creating separate brands to promote facets of its operations. Universities have done this for years: 'the Centre for This' and the 'Institute of That' are merely examples of brand proliferation. Schools may opt for specialist centres (a science & technology centre or an arts centre) or for the separation of age groups (a sixth form centre). The importance of separate brands is their ability to promote their individual USP thus adding to the attractions of the school, particularly where there might be some conflict with the general image the school wishes to promote. Thus a sixth form which wishes to promote the freedom and mature environment it offers may conflict with the more structured environment which the main school is promoting.

If the brand is recognised and has a positive image it is a valuable addition to the product and its augmentation. When a brand is not known or has negative connotations it will have the reverse effect. Schools might wish to 'borrow' the brand image of another organisation with which they are related but they must ensure it has the right *halo effect* on their image. For example, a strong link (perhaps through sponsorship or compacts) with a major local employer may have a positive effect if it is a leading manufacturer of high-quality products or a major financial services organisation; a chain of discount DIY warehouses, no matter how reputable, does not lend the same quality to the school.

Quality is probably the most important feature the product can possess. In Chapter 8 this will be dealt with in more detail but in rounding off this section it is worth emphasising that no amount of packaging, premium offers or branding can disguise poor-quality education for long, while good-quality education does its own marketing.

The problem of course is defining quality!

The product lifecycle

No product continues for ever; during its life, however short or long, it will need to be constantly updated. This is evident in the changes to the school curriculum that have regularly occurred. New syllabuses, new teaching and learning strategies, new subject areas, new exams; the process might seem endless. It is also difficult at times to know where the pressure for change has come from since, despite the switch to a market-oriented system of funding, curriculum control has become more and more centralised.

This latter phenomenon – the lack of control the school has over its core products – makes marketing in schools significantly different from marketing in most other sectors.

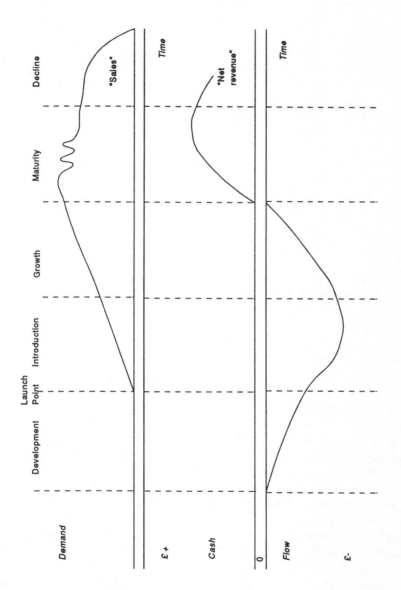

Figure 7.2 *The product lifecycle*

Despite this lack of direct control, the school has the power to interpret the curriculum to meet market needs and fit its own resource capability. It also has some freedom to determine whether or not to include certain products (vocational courses, for example, and those outside the statutory national curriculum). In developing new products or deleting old ones (wherever the pressure from change originates) it is useful to relate the process to the product lifecycle model. The product lifecycle is an analysis of the stages the product passes through during its life and predicts certain costs and decisions associated with those stages (see Figure 7.2).

The first stage is the development of the product, starting from the point that the first resources are committed to it. It is also the beginning of negative cash flow (shown in the lower half of the graph) as no revenue is being generated at this stage. The length of the development phase varies from product to product and industry to industry; in education it is not unusual for this phase to last for a year or more.

The launch of the product marks the beginning of the introduction to the market. This may be a *test market* (or pilot), where only a selected market group is exposed to the product and further development work takes place. Although revenue starts flowing at launch, the costs will often escalate as low volume, continuing development and initial promotion generates a substantial negative cash flow.

The introduction will usually have a slow start and there must be a sign of an upturn at a particular point for it to be evident that continued marketing is worthwhile. The hardest decision to make is to terminate a new product when substantial investment has already been made; the temptation must be to hang on just a bit longer to wait for a sign of growth. The establishment of success criteria at each key decision point (Are we ready to launch? Has the introduction been successful?) *before* the launch can help in making this decision.

The third stage, growth, occurs when the introduction has been successful. Marketing costs will still be high, but development costs should be tailing off and production economies should be occurring. The cash flow should now be bottoming out, with revenue and costs in balance, but a large deficit will have accumulated which is only eaten into as the growth stage moves into maturity. The product is now an established part of the product portfolio and should move into surplus, bringing in more revenue than it costs.

During the early part of maturity the accumulated deficit will have been paid back and the product starts making a contribution to the development of other products, until it starts moving into decline. When signs of decline start to appear, a decision must be made about whether or not to allow it to occur, or whether an attempt should be made to *relaunch* the product. This might include superficial changes to the core, repackaging and so on, or it may involve a fundamental redesign, with the original product providing little more than a skeleton for the relaunched version. The decision as to which strategy, if either, must depend on the market conditions; a small or short-life market would indicate the former, a potentially large or long-term market would justify the latter.

These *product extension strategies* are generally preferred to new product development because of the relatively high costs of development of both products and markets. An existing product has already enjoyed a substantial investment which is a *sunk cost* – it cannot be retrieved, but it can be used to generate future benefit. The alternative is to allow the product to go into decline, which is a perfectly valid marketing strategy and one which should be managed as consciously as a new product development. This means examining every opportunity to minimise costs, only committing enough resources to maintain the quality of the product and ensuring there is no wastage.

In particular, the criteria by which termination will be decided must be agreed; once the product reaches that point (which might be a point in time or a level of demand), it should be cut cleanly. A good product-portfolio-management strategy would have used the final stages of the product's life to support the development and introduction of replacement products to maintain a healthy portfolio.

One of the weaknesses of product management in education is a reluctance to allow declining products to die; they are continually supported by draining resources from mature products which would be put to better use developing new ones and supporting their introduction and growth. Equally there has been a tradition of funding new product development from external rather than internal sources. Systems of funding based on market demand will make both these practices less viable; schools will need to look at the stage on the product lifecycle which all products have reached and ensure that coherent strategies are developed to manage them.

The product lifecycle is not a guaranteed phenomenon: products may never progress from introduction to growth, or from growth to maturity. Decline may occur almost immediately the flattened demand occurs, with little or no period of maturity; alternatively, products may last for years with little more than maintenance needed to keep them going. Although the product lifecycle is a poor predictor of demand it is a useful model to be aware of to understand what is happening to the product and raise awareness of the options facing the manager.

Summary

Defining the product of education is problematic. From a marketing perspective, though, it is essential if the behaviour of the market is to be understood and influenced. The core product is just the beginning; marketing is concerned with the way that the core can be augmented to satisfy market demand. The way the product is packaged, branded and promoted determines the market perception.

Packaging is just as important for services as it is for goods; the range of services being offered can be presented separately or can be bundled together to form a coherent package for the market to choose. Various techniques are available to promote the product using premiums which are designed to 'add value' to it.

Pricing is not relevant to the majority of a school's activities, although some products (such as sweat-shirts) can be sold to contribute to school funds. However, the increasing ability of schools to offer non-statutory education services (nursery and adult education) makes pricing (and costing) a necessary marketing skill since the price charged reflects on the product. Branding can be used to influence perceptions of the product, to differentiate between products and to create an identity for the school.

The life of the product is likely to follow a pattern (the product lifecycle) which is predictable and which can be used to predict cash flow as well. As schools become more dependent on funding linked to actual enrolments they must be able to fund developments from their own resources, which means recognising that new products must be funded by mature ones. The product lifecycle clearly demonstrates the relationship between revenue and expenditure at different phases of the product's life.

Chapter 8

Developing New Products

Generating ideas

Where do new products come from? The number of changes in education over the last few years testifies to the number of ideas for new products; unfortunately most of them originate from outside schools. Certainly, major curriculum initiatives have tended to result from central government: TVEI, CPVE, GCSE and the like are the result of national policy decisions. However, many such initiatives have actually built on existing developments originating in schools, and many more arise in individual institutions or consortia, lacking only the limelight of national funding or support.

How, then, can new products be encouraged, stimulating innovation and enthusiasm for development within an overall portfolio of products at varying stages of the lifecycle? Innovation tends to rely on individuals or small groups, and there is an assumption that it occurs by chance, that it can't be managed. While it is true that some people are more able to generate new ideas, it is also true that creating the right (or wrong) environment can help (or hinder) the process of innovation. For the manager, creating the right environment, stimulating the process of innovation and providing sufficient resources to enable good ideas to prosper is a marketing function, essential to the long-term success of the organisation. Equally important, of course, is ensuring stability: good ideas cannot survive in a chaotic or unstable environment, and too much innovation can be as bad for an organisation as too little. Getting the balance right depends on good judgement, an awareness of individual and group capabilities, and the context in which people are working. Too few resources, a deteriorating physical environment, concern over pay and conditions; none of these are conducive to the generation of ideas.

Market information

It would be surprising if a book on marketing did not suggest that that new ideas should be generated by the market. Certainly, this should be the starting point, and the use of market research techniques (including simply talking to clients) is always going to be a valuable source of ideas. Pupils may want more vocational courses, more applied subjects, greater integration. These ideas can provide the initial impetus for new product development.

External institutions

However, such market information may only give a vague sense of the kind of new products required; it is often insufficient to allow immediate development work to be undertaken. Frequently, market needs must be matched to ideas being generated elsewhere outside the school, by higher education institutions or examination boards keen to stimulate curriculum developments in particular areas. These sources can be thought of as the equivalent of research institutes in manufacturing industry, coming up with novel products and searching for a use. Such an approach should not be scorned – an attempt to find a use for an adhesive which didn't stick led the 3M company to market 'Post-its'!

Competition

A third source of new ideas is competitors; other schools may well have already developed the new product which meets market need. Using somebody else's ideas is a perfectly legitimate strategy. The biggest problem any organisation has in undertaking a 'me too' strategy (and also with taking on outside research ideas) is overcoming the 'not invented here' syndrome, the rejection of other people's ideas simply because they were not originated in-house. The simplest solution is to personalise the idea, putting your own stamp on it so that it no longer belongs elsewhere; the enthusiasm of staff can be harnessed by establishing such 'ownership'.

Internal procedures

The generation of ideas for new products from the market, external institutions or competitors will also need to be augmented by internal procedures, to expand such ideas or to provide an alternative source. Such procedures can be fairly simple or they can involve complex processes, perhaps mediated by external consultants. What is certain is that leaving it to chance is a good strategy for minimising the process. There may be a minority of innovators who will produce good ideas under any circumstances. There are also many people working in schools who are innovative and able to contribute new ideas, but they need some support and encouragement to voice those ideas and progress them outside their existing area of activity and sphere of influence.

Making the process of generating ideas a formalised procedure has three benefits:

- it enables people with ideas to advance them in an environment which is welcoming and supportive (or should be) rather than negative and discouraging;
- it values staff and gives them a chance to 'own' developments, even when they have been initiated outside the school or by its management;
- it ensures that programmes for future development can also be planned, to avoid leaving the progressing of such new ideas to chance or a single enthusiast.

Some of the techniques for stimulating new ideas are not particularly novel; the most widely known and used is *brainstorming*, developed some 30 years ago as a problem-solving technique in the advertising agency BBDO. A similar though more complex approach, which requires the mediation of an experienced group leader, is the use of *synectics*, a technique developed by William Gordon. Whereas brainstorming relies on speed of suggestion, free association, the absence of structure, and the quantity of ideas generated to provoke solutions to a problem, synectics has a more structured approach which avoids the specific problem and addresses it as a general issue, using existing solutions to parallel problems and metaphors to stimulate unconventional viewpoints, working away at a problem steadily over quite extended periods of time. (See Figure 8.1)

Other techniques are used in a variety of training and development contexts (brain maps, morphological analysis and the like) and they are all valuable in stimulating new ideas and approaches. The key to

Problem	Pupils need more variety in their learning experiences.
Brainstorming	Creates a list of ideas spontaneously suggested by the problem.

- Different subjects
- Shorter periods, more subjects in a day
- Interactive video
- Workshops

- Projects
- Resource-based learning
- Staff development

Synectics	May address the issue through a consideration of variety in a different context (= What is variety?)

- Variety shows – singing, dancing, juggling comedians, etc
- Variety shops – open plan with areas given over to different goods, etc
- Variety sweets – different colours, flavours, textures, etc

Figure 8.1 *Brainstorming and synectics approaches*

success for any procedure is that it is supported by managers and not constrained by immediately identifying all the problems of implementation. The *lateral thinking* approach encouraged by Edward de Bono relies on allowing ideas to be pursued in unconventional and apparently inappropriate directions, producing solutions which can often make far more effective use of existing resources.

Screening

Generating new ideas is the first half of the *design phase* of new product development; *screening* is the second half. The generation of new ideas relies on maximising the number; the rest of the process is about eliminating them. The majority are lost through screening, where new ideas are evaluated for their *viability* and *validity*. Viability is concerned with the ability of the organisation to sustain the idea (can we do it?); validity is concerned with its ability to meet market demand (do they want it?). The 3 × 3 Matrix (Figure 3.5 on page 63) is an example of a business screen which can be used to test new ideas for viability and validity, with 'market validity' substituted for 'market attractiveness'.

The ideal new-product design phase will involve the generation of a substantial number of new ideas subsequently honed down to a manageable number during the screening process. Obvious non-starters (for reasons of inadequate resources, unsuitability for the market, inappropriateness to the school's mission, or an alternative provider having market dominance) can be whittled out easily. Harder decisions might need to be made about several viable alternatives when adequate resources exist for only one. However, the purpose of screening is not to eliminate all but one idea: the development phase can accommodate several ideas, some of which will not be progressed to implementation. The screen should be used primarily to eliminate those which are clearly unlikely to be viable or valid.

However, in eliminating some ideas and allowing others to go ahead it is important to avoid two kinds of error. *NO GO* errors occur when an organisation dismisses an otherwise good idea because of a lack of vision. Those unconventional ideas which challenge existing ways of working or which would involve changes in institutional structures or which cannot easily be visualised in operation should not be dismissed without careful thought. The purpose of new product development is not to reproduce existing provision but to introduce innovation.

GO errors occur when poor ideas are allowed through the screen to development and implementation; they can lead to *product failures*. Product failures are the 'really good ideas' which nobody wanted to buy, often with advanced technical features but without market need. Classic product failures in the UK have included BR's tilting high-speed train and the Sinclair C5 electric vehicle. Some product failures stem from technical failure (they just don't work to specification) but these should be rare and should be eliminated during the development phase. The majority fail because there is insufficient demand. That does not make them market failures; it is not the market's fault if it doesn't want the product, no matter how much it *should* want it!

Product failures tend to fall into three categories:

- *absolute* product failures, which flop immediately and never progress beyond introduction;

- *partial* product failures, which generate enough demand to progress beyond introduction but which have a flattened growth, are always marginal and will have a short life;
- *relative* product failures, which develop through to maturity and are judged to fail through comparison with other products, similar products provided by other organisations, or expectations of the product's demand.

Clearly NO GO errors are often unknown, unless another provider is successful with an idea which was screened out; *GO* errors become apparent at various stages in the product lifecycle according to their nature. The purpose of screening is to minimise both types of error and to reduce the ideas generated in the first part of the design phase to a level that can be progressed through to the development phase (see Figure 8.2).

The outcome of the screening process is a set of *ideas* for products, not the products themselves. The purpose of the design phase is to maximise the number of ideas by minimising the level of detail contained in them. Once those ideas have been screened for viability and validity, the freedom to be creative has to be tempered by the need to ensure that practical details can be worked out. During the concept development, the emphasis must be placed on market perceptions of the product: What practical experiences will the market have? what will be the implications for them of selecting this product? What outcomes can they expect? It is also important to define the market or market segment accurately so that these perceptions can be identified accurately.

Concept development and testing

The purpose of concept development is to identify the core product, not to attempt to identify strategies for augmenting it. It is too easy to get sidetracked into discussions about how the product will be presented to the market when the core is still little more than a good idea. Once a clear concept has been developed it is useful to establish how it relates to other products in the portfolio (*portfolio positioning*) and similar products from other providers (*competitive positioning*). A school which has decided to develop a new curriculum offer, generated

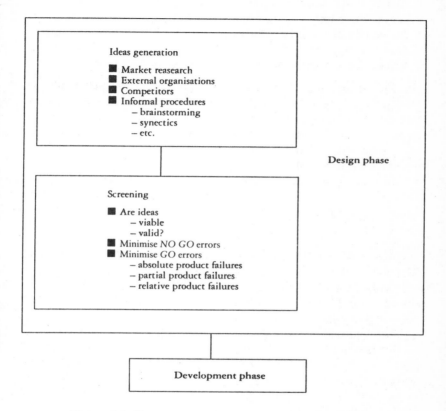

Figure 8.2 *New product development: design phase*

a number of ideas and screened these down to a few likely products and refined them into coherent product concepts must now decide where they each fit into its existing curriculum provision. It must also look at other schools and judge its relationship to their curriculum. Is this a distinctive concept which provides a unique feature for the school which distinguishes it from others? Or is it a 'me too' product, to minimise the product advantage of others?

It is also sensible at this stage to test the concept in the market to check how well it meets market needs, a secondary screening to minimise GO errors. The market must be asked:

- how well the concept is understood;
- how it compares to alternative products in the portfolio;
- how it compares to products from alternative providers;
- whether they would choose this product;
- what improvements they would like to see in the product.

Focus groups and semi-structured (not using questionnaires but guided to cover relevant topics) one-to-one interviews are a sensible strategy to adopt. If a school believes in being pupil-centred in its curriculum, market-centred in its orientation, and it if wishes to make its new product development as effective and resource-efficient as possible, the testing of concepts at this stage is crucial.

Market analysis and resourcing

Having developed the idea into a concept, a core product, which has been tested in the market and has shown itself viable and valid, it is now appropriate to undertake a review of its market potential and the resource implications of undertaking further development and implementation.

The viability of the idea has been established by looking at the ability of the school to provide the product; that is, the school has the resources (the staff, the rooms, the equipment and so on) – even though they may already be fully committed – or can acquire or get access to those resources. It is now necessary to quantify the resource implications of the product:

- How far would the product utilise spare capacity?
- How far would the product require the redeployment of existing resources?
- How much development of existing resources would be required?
- What other provision would be affected by the redeployment and development of existing resources?
- What new resources would be required?

In order to determine the answer to these questions, some idea is needed of the level of demand to enable the size of provision to be estimated. The validity of the product in the market has been tested to establish that the market is likely to be attracted to it; now it is necessary to establish how large that *potential market* is, and how large a share of the market the product is likely to achieve (its expected *market penetration*).

Market potential is easy to define but hard to measure; market penetration is also easy to define, but even harder to predict. The need for high-quality market information (as emphasised in Chapter 6) becomes apparent; a product which is designed for a particular market segment which the school has failed to attract now needs to have the market potential quantified. How large is that market segment? What is the number of potential pupils? The school knows it probably won't recruit all of them, but they are the potential market. Deciding how large that potential market is (who *could* take up this product offer?) provides the school with an idea of the maximum possible take-up.

Predicting market penetration (the proportion of the potential market expected to take up the product offer) involves making estimates about the level of demand within the potential market relative to alternative products and providers and the effectiveness of the school's promotion of its new product. Such estimates will be based on past experience, the earlier testing of the product concept, and the school's confidence in its own ability to develop and market a new product effectively.

Given the lifespan of most educational products, and the fact that each product involves a participation cycle of at least one year and up to six years, predicting market potential and penetration must involve the school in estimating its commitment for several years ahead. Using the checklist in Figure 1.1 (page 20), decisions related to new product development are likely to be strategic decisions. The timespan, the complexity of the problems involved, the information need, frequency of the activity, the level at which final decisions will need to be made, all point to the importance of the issues being dealt with.

Product development

The idea has been generated and screened, the concept developed, the market analysed and resourcing implications identified; now is the time to make a major decision – whether to go ahead – since the next part of the development process involves the first major commitment of resources. The product concept (a description of the core product) has to be converted into a product reality (a partially augmented product).

A detailed description of the finished product – the experiences that the pupil will have – needs to be constructed, including: of

- the knowledge and skills to be developed;
- the nature of the learning experiences;
- a plan of the learning process.

These should be developed and presented in a form as near as possible to the product as it will be experienced by the learner. Apart from types of resource-based learning packages, this is difficult to achieve since most teaching is difficult to simulate. However, a description of the product, with some parts in great detail to give as full a picture as possible of the nature of the experience, will suffice.

To use an example, a product development may be a new programme of work experience for pupils; although this cannot be simulated, a description of the process (briefing, placement selection, a typical placement programme, teacher visits, placement report, placement follow-ups in classwork) will enable managers to visualise the experience. Furthermore, it will give pupils a chance to comment on the product in repeats of the testing procedures used for the concept.

It is also important to identify the ways in which the core product will be augmented. How will the product be packaged? What promotional strategies will be used to stimulate demand? What brand image and brand name are appropriate to attract participants and encapsulate what the product is about?

It is also appropriate to initiate the resource development or acquisition needed to implement the product. Staff must be trained, rooms converted, materials and equipment made ready or acquired. The labour intensity of the education process puts a premium on staff development when new products are being developed. Learning new techniques, preparing new support materials and making new contacts, all form part of the process. Training contributes to this and enables staff development to occur. However there is far more to staff development than just training.

The development phase, therefore, consists of three elements:

- concept development and testing;
- market analysis and resourcing;
- product development.

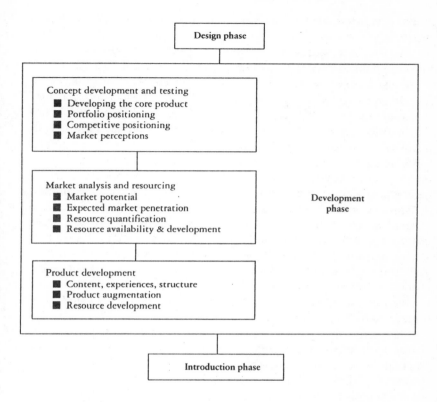

Figure 8.3 *New product development: development phase*

The initial design phase produces the ideas; the development phase converts them into products which are ready to move into the third phase: introduction. (See Figure 8.3)

Test marketing

It is all too easy to launch a new product as a fully fledged member of the product portfolio, expecting it to perform as well as the other existing products as if the development phase is now completed. Up till now the development and testing of the ideas, the concepts and product have been 'laboratory' based, that is, the new product has not been presented to the market in a form and context in which mainstream products are marketed. The test market is an opportunity to do this but to recognise that the process is still one where development can occur and *precedes* the final decision to launch.

A test market (which in education is often called a pilot) is an opportunity to offer a new product to the market in a tightly constrained way. The level of provision is limited (the product is not yet in 'full production') and the market selected is a readily defined but representative sub-set of the total market. Most education pilots observe this first criterion but often neglect the second, choosing a market segment which is most likely to want and/or benefit from the product and which is, therefore, unrepresentative of the total market.

This latter error was often apparent during the 1980s when the Technical and Vocational Education Initiative (TVEI) was being piloted. Although intended to be a development aimed at all segments of the market, it was not uncommon for those groups most likely to proceed into vocational education or employment at 16 (the middle ability quartiles) to be recruited. This made subsequent extension across the whole market difficult as the product had been tested on an unrepresentative sample.

The motive for test marketing is simple: it enables the producer to ensure that the product is right and to assess its market potential more accurately. Thus the reactions of those who have chosen the new product, and the reactions of those who haven't, are important in identifying those facets of the new product which have influenced their choice decision. One advantage that education has over many other sectors, particularly manufacturing, is that the product can undergo 'running repairs' to respond to the reactions of the market. A disadvantage of education is the high degree of ownership which teachers have for their 'products'; the commitment which they have to their pupils can too easily be transferred to their courses, making them resistant to changing the product.

The test market must therefore be defined quite clearly as a developmental process where change is not discouraged and where *not* changing has to be justified. This shifting of the emphasis away from having to justify change to having to justify maintaining the product as tested encourages the staff involved in development to examine the market reaction. Techniques for monitoring market reaction can include the use of questionnaires and group discussion to provide feedback from pupils, with regular evaluation of the response to assess the changes needed to ensure the product meets market needs.

The most important outcome of the test market is the decision whether or not to move to the full launch; the GO/NO GO decision must be made consciously at a designated stage against predetermined criteria.

Both these elements of the decision are essential if the test market is to be of value. There is a tendency in education to expect new products to be successful, partly to justify the initial development costs, and for the extension from pilot to full implementation (test market to launch) to occur by default. Establishing that at an identified time in the test market, and against identified criteria, the product will proceed to full launch, be discontinued, or move back into further development, is the principle purpose of test marketing.

Establishing the time when this decision needs to be made will depend on the institution's own planning cycles and the nature of the provision involved. The criteria by which the decision will be made should start from the market, using quantitative and qualitative feedback from the product's 'consumers' to assess how well the product has achieved its (market) objectives. Has it achieved the level of take-up expected and have the pupils completed the course successfully (or do they appear likely to)? In addition to such quantitative indicators, what qualitative indicators are there that it has met their needs and how does this compare to the teachers' own perceptions of their reactions? Only when the school is confident that the test market has shown that the new product is capable of achieving its objectives (perhaps with modification) should the full launch be contemplated.

Launching the new product

The launch of a new product is the point at which it joins the full product portfolio and moves from the responsibility of a developmental group to the responsibility of those who will manage and deliver it. These may in fact be the same people, but their role is now changed; by signalling this change it is possible to establish that new criteria are now in operation for assessing the resourcing requirements and market response.

In terms of the product lifecycle, the product is now well into its introductory phase and should be approaching the period of growth which precedes maturity. It will still be a net drain on resources compared to other mature products and still requires particular monitoring to ensure its long-term success. However, the transfer of responsibility (however nominal) from a development group to the mainstream is a way of reducing the higher costs and releasing resources for developments elsewhere.

The full new-product development process (design, development and introduction) is a long-term activity which needs to be seen from a strategic perspective. The need to balance resources between different curriculum areas, to manage an activity which will occur over years rather than months, and which may well shift the direction and culture of the institution if the new product is substantially different from existing products, will all involve strategic decisions. It is often the failure to appreciate the strategic significance of new products which prejudices their success or inhibits them from achieving their full potential. In particular, senior managers can all too easily focus their attention on maintaining mature or declining products on the assumption that responsibility for a new product has been delegated to a project team or leader.

Such an approach demonstrates its weakness most keenly during the introduction, particularly at the full launch of the new product, when the implications of the developments become apparent for the whole organisation and resistance manifests itself. An addition to the curriculum of a school, particularly one which involves a substantial shift in the pattern of provision, often represents a substantial challenge to the balance of power, the culture and the working practices of other staff. Without the support of senior managers, the resources devoted to such a development may well be wasted. Now that such resources are increasingly having to be found from within existing budgets, rather than being provided by education authorities, schools must ensure their commitment is real. However, by adopting the procedures outlined in this chapter (see Figure 8.4) managers can have more confidence that they will be able to increase the effectiveness and efficiency with which resources are deployed in new product development.

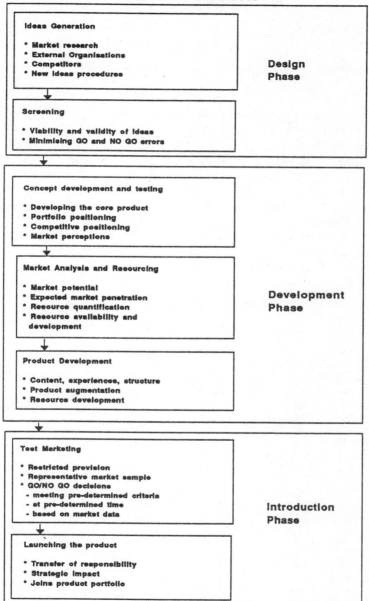

Figure 8.4 *The three phases of new product development*

Summary

New product ideas can be developed from a number of sources: from the market, from research by external institutions, from competitors and from within the school. Deliberately setting out to look for new ideas is an essential part of new product development. These can then be screened for their suitability and concepts developed and tested in the market.

Once a market has been established and the resourcing implications of the new product clarified, the concept can be developed into a product for test marketing. Only when this has shown the effectiveness of the product and the scale of market demand should the product be launched.

This framework for product development enables the process to be managed, the market to be established, resources to be deployed efficiently and wastage minimised.

Chapter 9

Managing the Product Portfolio

The product portfolio: the product/market mix

The notion of a product portfolio has been developed from the investment portfolio model which encourages investors to spread their investments across a range of businesses to ensure that risks are minimised. For the product portfolio the same principles apply: minimising risk by ensuring that an organisation is not fully committed to a limited range of markets and products. Where economies of scale or minimum economic size make such a spread difficult, joint ventures and consortia enable such risk-reduction strategies to be undertaken. Thus the key objective – minimising risk – is achieved by a combination of *product spread* and *market spread*.

The product spread is the prime characteristic of the product portfolio; it is the organisation's range of products which is usually identified as its product portfolio. The range can be identified as being a set of distinctive and separate core products, or it may consist of a single or limited set of core products that have been extensively augmented to enable the narrow base of core products to be presented as a wide range of differentiated products through the use of promotional, packaging and branding strategies.

The larger the potential market and the lower the costs in setting up new production facilities, the greater are the opportunities for expanding the core product base. A limited market size may make it difficult to achieve economies of scale (the savings from large-scale production) or to reach the minimum economic size (the smallest size at which effective production is possible). The higher the entry costs (the costs of setting up new production) the higher are the risks for an organisation penetrating a new market. Thus it makes sense in smaller markets or those where high entry costs exist to expand the product range by augmenting core products rather than producing new products.

In this context, augmentation can be defined broadly as the set of variations in the core product which enable distinctive and separate products to be created. Often this can involve minimal variation in the physical core but extensive variation in its packaging, promotion, distribution, pricing and branding. This is particularly valuable where a range of market segments exist, each of which has significant differences in its demand. It is this characteristic which distinguishes the notion of product portfolio from product range: the latter is product defined, the former is also defined in terms of its markets and by those networks of promotion and distribution which link the products to their markets (see Figure 9.1).

The reduction of risk offered by expanding the product portfolio is dependent on both the market and product spread. Variation in the demand for different types of product and fluctuations in the level of demand between different markets can both be accommodated by a broadly based product portfolio. The greater the dependence on a single product or market, the higher the risks from relatively minor changes in demand.

Niche marketing

There are some circumstances, however, where it might be inappropriate for an organisation to consider expanding across more than a limited range of products because of the high degree of specialisation dictated by the production process. This may require a high capital investment and the recruitment of a highly skilled labour force, neither of which can easily be transferred to alternative production activities. Equally, the market which is being targeted might have such particular characteristics that only a high level of involvement through market contact and knowledge enable it to be penetrated, making it difficult

The product portfolio is defined by reference to the variety in its core and augmented products, the market segments and the networks which link the products and markets.

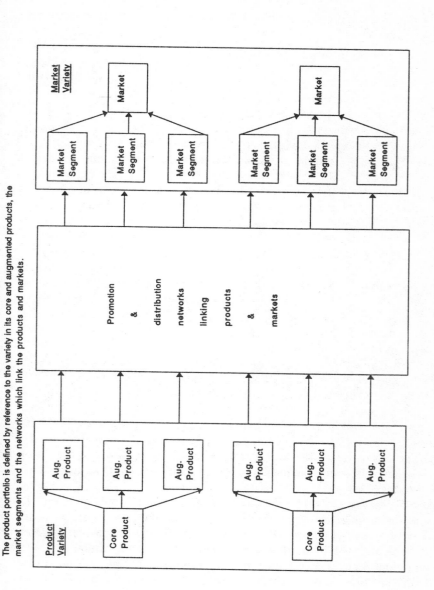

Figure 9.1 *The product portfolio*

for an organisation not wholly dedicated to that market to penetrate it effectively.

At this extreme, therefore, the organisation might be engaged in *niche marketing* with a narrow product range or even a single product. The market niche is usually defined as a small but distinctive market which is only able to sustain a limited or single source of supply because of the specialist knowledge or production operations involved. These act as *barriers to entry* to new suppliers, enabling existing, dominant, suppliers to enjoy a monopolistic advantage. Where the capital cost of entry is high (through the need for expensive equipment dedicated only to producing a product for this market), the existing suppliers might also have *barriers to exit*. Their *sunk costs* (the costs of specialist capital) are not recoverable if they leave the market – their capital has no alternative applications.

Appreciating the characteristics of such a market position is important since the strengths of the organisation, of limited competition and market dominance, may also generate weaknesses through the limitations on manoeuvre they present to its management. A specialist, niche, marketing strategy may offer protection from competitive action but it may also limit the options open to the organisation, inhibiting new product development and market expansion.

Such an extreme form of niche marketing is unlikely to occur where the market is a segment of a larger market, rather than a distinctive market in its own right. (Of course, in practice, these distinctions are of degree rather than of kind. A market segment may be only just definable within a predominantly homogeneous market, or it may be so distinctive as to be regarded as a separate market in its own right.) The fewer the distinctive characteristics of the market and the lower the entry barriers, the harder it is for an organisation to sustain such a strategy.

To be successful in niche marketing, the market must be definable by the supplier and recognised by its members. If the market occupants are not conscious of belonging to a particular market or market segment, it will be harder to communicate with them effectively or to prevent their 'straying' into other markets and accepting competitive offers. Conversely, the protectiveness of the market towards its own distinctiveness might be the only characteristic which distinguishes it. The members are so conscious of their commonality that they ignore their similarities with other markets or market segments, and their demand for a unique product or set of products is essentially a requirement for a distinctively branded product rather than one which is distinctive as a *core* product.

The niche market, with its single product supplier, is one extreme of a complex mix of product and market spread, both of which can be increased until the organisation is fully diversified, having a product portfolio which reflects the maximum variation in its customers and the goods and services it supplies. This range of options is illustrated in Figure 9.2. For the managers of an organisation, the ability to identify where they are and where they should be on these two dimensions is essential. Planning the product portfolio is the core of the organisation's marketing strategy and determines its long-term success.

Most schools will lie somewhere around the middle of the diagram in Figure 9.2. Their market is not exclusively drawn from one segment, nor is it singularly distinctive from the market which other schools are supplying. Equally, the range of products which they offer is wide but does not extend beyond an essentially related range of teaching and learning strategies, although a few schools may limit themselves to a unique product or very limited range of products. However, within the parameters of product and market spread appropriate to schools, there are possibilities for moving towards one or other of the four strategies identified in Figure 9.2. Which strategy is pursued depends upon the market opportunities, the institution's abilities and its mission. The analysis of the first two was explored in Chapter 2, and the importance of the mission (the school's aims and values) was emphasised in Chapter 1.

Specialist product/diverse market strategy

The City Technology Colleges (CTCs) were originally advocated as offering a technologically oriented curriculum, centred on science and information technology with a vocational slant, but capable of meeting the needs of a diverse market. Thus they would cater for all ability ranges, community sectors and for both sexes, with larger catchment areas than traditional secondary education has had. This strategy, which involves specialising in the product range coupled with an intention to aim for market diversity, is most appropriate where

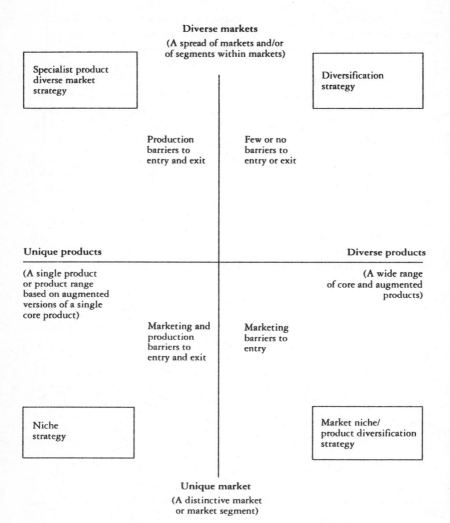

Figure 9.2 *The product/market mix*

production costs inhibit the development of a broad product range. If the curriculum provision of CTCs requires a degree of specialisation in capital and staff which is appropriate for a wide range of pupils, it can be classified as fitting this particular category of product/market mix in its product portfolio.

The difficulty in education is ensuring that specialisation in curriculum provision does not at the same time have the effect of narrowing the market spread. Traditionally, there has been a tendency for different curriculum areas to attract particular groups: girls, in languages, boys in the physical sciences for example. Thus the social pressures in the market place shape perceptions of the curriculum and influence decisions between the options available. For a school which decides to embark on a strategy of product specialisation and market diversity in its product portfolio, there are distinct hurdles to be overcome. Failing to recognise these hurdles and preparing for them with a marketing strategy which sets out deliberately to compensate for the inherent tendencies of the market may lead to the school having a *de facto* niche-marketing strategy.

The importance of market information cannot be underestimated in this context; if the intention is to specialise in the product mix while maintaining market diversity, that market must be clearly identified and classified. Identifying the market and its various characteristics will enable the school to:

- prepare promotional strategies appropriate to the various market segments and designed to counteract inherent preferences which will distort demand;
- measure the effectiveness of its market diversity strategy by mapping the actual market against the potential market to identify distortions.

One problem to be recognised is that any strategy which intentionally or unintentionally gives preference to one group in the population over another may well lead to prosecution under sex- or race- equality legislation. In particular, any attempt to set entry criteria which are different for one group from another, or which inherently favour one group over another may be classed as inequitable. It is for this reason that to achieve diversity in the school population, the school must focus on the promotional strategies which influence demand rather than on trying to engineer the market diversity through entry procedures. Targeting minority groups in promotion is a legitimate tactic to pursue to ensure participation is spread across the population; setting entry quotas is not.

Niche strategy

A tightly targeted market for a tightly defined product represents the extreme form of niche marketing. For a school, such a strategy can be arrived at by accident or it can occasionally be an intentional outcome. Most commonly, niche marketing is found in the private sector where schools have set out deliberately to establish themselves as providers of a highly specialised form of education (in music or dance, for example), where the requirement for particular facilities or staff is matched by a highly selective recruitment strategy. The narrowness of the market being targeted, in terms of the abilities required by those being recruited (as well as the ability to pay) can become a dominant feature of the school's promotional strategy. The barriers to entry erected by the school become part of its attraction.

Such approaches have been considered in the public sector, with the magnet school model. Although not emphasising quite such an exclusivity in the recruiting strategies as suggested above, the notion of the magnet school is an example of a niche marketing strategy. A product specialism is coupled with a market base defined primarily by its interest or ability in that particular curriculum area. The logic of the magnet school is that by concentrating on one curriculum area, investing in appropriate capital and recruiting appropriate staff, the school can raise the overall standard of educational provision. Pupils attracted to such a school by their enthusiasm for the subject(s) would be better motivated and thus benefit from its facilities. However, unless the school is prepared to operate a system of selection which focuses on ability or potential in that curriculum area (its market definition) it will be unable to produce the level of outcomes which would justify such an investment. For this reason the school's promotional strategy would need to focus on the particular market segment(s) most likely to be potential pupils. It would also need to feature the selectivity of its intake in order to be able to have a convincing logic for its specialisation.

A third area of niche marketing occurs where a school for those with special educational needs (its target market) concentrates on particular curriculum areas, such as basic skills or preparing pupils for particular occupational or functional activities. Such a combination of product and market mix is determined by the specific needs of a tightly defined market segment. It must be stressed that the specialist product in a 'pure' niche strategy is more about emphasis on a specialism within a diverse product range rather than subject exclusivity, since all schools need to provide a full curriculum offer (particularly to meet the needs of the National Curriculum).

Market niche/diverse product strategy

The logic of targeting a particular market while offering an otherwise generic product range lies in the way that such a product range is presented. It is the augmentation of the core product to meet the particular demands of the target market which 'camouflages' a generic offer to make it appear specialist.

Such a strategy has been a common feature of the British education system in the voluntary aided (VA) denominational schools, which are established to meet the needs of particular religious sectors of the market while offering a product range often little different from that of other schools, except for a clear statement about the dominant ethic shaping the institutional culture.

There has been pressure to extend this provision to include a wider range of denominations and religions to reflect the increasing diversity of the society which education serves. Given that many of these schools would offer little different in the way of a core product (given the requirements for a school wanting to have VA status and the demands of the National Curriculum), they can be defined primarily by their market focus rather than a product focus.

Many schools have practised a niche market/diverse product strategy by default as much as by design. The existence of a naturally defined catchment area due to geography and transport arrangements, traditional links with feeder schools, the school's history and its location in a particular residential area, can lead to the market being restricted to a particular segment or group of market segments. These latter two factors are particularly important in the case of comprehensive schools, which have converted from either grammar or secondary

modern status. Their origins and their proximity to particular neigh-
bourhoods determine their propensity to recruit from particular social
classes. Without deliberate strategies to counteract such tendencies,
the school will continue to recruit from its narrow base and to reinforce
stereotyped images held of it.

Diversification strategy

Most schools aim, as far as possible, to offer the widest product range
to the widest number of market segments. Such a strategy reflects their
definition of their community purpose as much as a considered analysis
of the market. However, it is always valid to question such strategies
when a competitive situation exists, since the provision of choice
enables a school to determine how valid it is for it to attempt to satisfy
all market demand.

Of course, it is almost impossible to satisfy the whole market; most
schools have to set priorities and will generally aim to produce the
maximum range of products to satisfy the maximum number of people.
Questioning a diversification strategy is as much about the basis on
which the strategy operates (including what has been left out of the
product portfolio, either by accident or design) as it is to question the
principle underlying it.

In an input-funded system, attempts to ensure that all market
segments are offered the widest possible range of provision can easily
lead to pressures for uniformity. By ensuring that all schools follow
similar curriculum strategies and pursue common goals the outcome
might be achieved. In an output funded system, such strategies may
not necessarily be either necessary or useful. The pressure on
institutions to respond to market needs is more likely to encourage
differentiation than uniformity. Thus, ensuring that individuals have
maximum choice of opportunities might be best achieved by encouraging institutional diversity and specialisation, with the market choosing
between institutions to achieve their goals rather than having maximum choice within each.

Such an argument presupposes three conditions:

- there is choice between institutions (ie, competition rather than
  monopoly);

- the institutions use differentiation rather than 'me too' strategies when specialising, so that there is real choice;
- that between the differentiated institutions there exists as wide a range of choice as would occur if each institution aimed at maximum diversity.

Achieving these conditions depends in part on the attitudes prevailing within the appropriate group of institutions and in part on the funding regime and the extent to which it enables variety across the institutions rather than assuming it must occur within each. It also, of course, depends on the logistics of the situation: where a single school based in a county town with an extensive rural hinterland is the only choice available, diversification is an essential prerequisite for any meaningful choice to be available to the market.

Ensuring maximum opportunity to the market does not, therefore, necessarily require all schools to adopt diversification strategies. The specialisation in product offerings and targeting of market segments outlined above can, if sufficient numbers of schools exist, ensure that the market is well served with choice. However, where an individual school has decided to undertake a diversification strategy, it is able to enjoy the benefits of risk minimisation if the strategy is effective. Its vulnerability to changes in demand is reduced as it has a range of markets and products, not all of which are likely to be affected and some of which may well benefit from the shifts in demand.

The greater the flexibility of resources, the more a diversification strategy is sustainable as it ensures that the school can respond quickly to market changes. Also, the larger the institution, the more likely it will be to sustain an effective diversification strategy. Largeness enables the minimum economic size of any particular aspect of the curriculum to be achieved (to justify the existence of specialist resources, for example, which are not underused or used for alternative purposes). Size is obviously relative, and a school must make a judgement about the level of flexibility of its resources and the minimum size it needs to be to justify their existence.

It is also necessary to consider the extent to which an increase in the product range will generate additional demand rather than subdivide existing demand, making that which was previously viable no longer so. A school which decides to expand and strengthen its science and technology provision by adding a laboratory and workshop to its existing resources and taking on new staff, enabling it to offer a wider range of subjects, may well find that one consequence is to subdivide existing demand without generating extra. Establishing that there is a potential market, identifying its particular requirements and considering the impact on the existing market of new products, is clearly important when engaging in a diversification strategy.

Deciding the product portfolio strategy

Which way should a school go? Should it focus its efforts on a niche market or should it aim for the widest possible range of market segments? Should it aim to specialise in a few product areas to enjoy some competitive edge, or aim to offer the maximum curriculum range it can? The choice depends on the market and the school's ability to respond. The mechanisms for reaching the decision are a combination of analysis of the market and the school, and the judgement of managers.

In Chapter 3, some of the analytical tools available to facilitate decision-making were examined:

- SWOT analysis;
- the Ansoff matrix;
- the BCG matrix;
- the Business Screen (3 × 3) matrix.

Each one can contribute to the process of coherent assessment of the potential opportunities and the ability of the school to exploit them. The schools 'strengths and weaknesses' and the market's 'opportunities and threats' provide the initial assessment. The Ansoff matrix highlights the range of options and, in the process, focuses attention on the choices. Both the BCG and the Business Screen matrix force judgements to be made about the situation, both within the school and in its environment.

None of these will substitute for effective managers since the quality of the data being fed into the decision-making process is dependent upon their ability to collect and analyse that data. Furthermore, none of these analytical tools is a decision-making tool in itself; what they can do is to highlight the options and predicate the outcomes of particular strategies. It is the managers' responsibility to make the final decisions, balancing the outcomes of the process against their own knowledge, experience and willingness to take risks. There is only one certainty – the decision not taken is always the wrong one!

Quality and the product portfolio

The shift of funding from inputs to outputs has caused education authorities to focus attention on the nature of the outputs of the education process. Defining those outputs quantitatively is problematic enough but pales into insignificance when the issue of quality is introduced. It is not just a question of how much output is being funded, but of how good that output is.

A variety of indicators have been proposed to measure qualitative performance; all suffer from the difficulty of defining quality in education in a way which lends itself to objective assessment and validation. Why is this relevant to marketing? Because the judgement of the market on the quality of provision by a school is the ultimate evaluation and the only one which matters in the long run. If the market is not convinced of the quality of a school, the gradual decline in recruitment which results will be far more influential than the judgements of funders, no matter how authoritative.

The industrial definition of quality – 'fitness for purpose' – is not one which necessarily appeals to educators, who prefer to think of quality in terms of 'excellence'. The former is seen as the minimum acceptable standard or utility, the latter is aspirational, towards a maximum standard, however unattainable.

The value of the 'fitness for purpose' approach to quality is, however, that it encourages the provider to focus on market perceptions and demands. What is expected from the school and how well does it perform in meeting marketing perceptions? Such questions are especially pertinent when considering the product portfolio since:

- the quality of individual products reflects on the whole portfolio;
- the range of products will, in itself, define the quality of the portfolio in the perceptions of the market;
- the ability of the school to provide and sustain a particular portfolio will shape perceptions of the quality of the institution.

A product portfolio is as good as the weakest element in that portfolio; a school which offers a wide range of successful products, well received by the market and perceived as 'high quality', will find that a failure impacts on all of them. A market failure can depress demand for other products; a quality failure can taint other products. Just as a teacher is only as good as the last lesson, or a manager as good as the last decision, so a product portfolio is only as good as the poorest-quality product in the eyes of others.

It is also important to appreciate how important it is to many in the market that a school can offer choices, even when the individuals may have no intention of taking those choices. The range of product offerings is seen as part of the quality of provision; for the school which intends to specialise, this perception of quality has to be overcome by being able to make some concrete demonstration of the quality of its speciality. This perception of breadth of curriculum as indication of quality is, in part, a reflection of the difficulty of demonstrating educational quality without actually experiencing the school's curriculum offer. Offering a range of activities (both intra- and extra-curricular) can act as a proxy for the quality of the institutional offer.

This third dimension is the most important aspect of market choice; it is not the individual products or the whole portfolio which are being chosen, but the school. The quality of the institution, as perceived by the market, is a result of a combination of factors, where the whole is often greater than the sum of its parts. From the paintwork on the windows to the ability of its staff, the market's judgement about the school's quality will determine how effective its marketing effort will be. No amount of promotion will overcome poor teaching, in the long run; the school which is renowned for the quality of its provision has its reputation as its principal promotional vehicle. Ensuring that the products in its portfolio, and the portfolio as a whole, project the right image for the school and that the reality of those products and that portfolio match up to that image is the core of the school's marketing.

Summary

The range of products and the diversity of the market segments the school is targeting are the main elements in its product-portfolio strategy. The advantages of a wide range of products and markets, by minimising risk, must be contrasted against the attractions of a niche-marketing strategy.

The combinations of specialist or diverse products and niche or diverse markets provide the four main portfolio-strategy options open to a school. It must make a decision about which it is to pursue based upon the use of marketing information, their analysis and the judgement of the managers. Above all else, it must ensure that the school's overall aims and values are adhered to.

The quality of the school's provision is a major dimension of the product portfolio, and the perception of the market is the key to determining the nature of quality. In a market-oriented system, understanding the market's perception of quality is essential in deciding on what the school should offer and how it should be promoted.

PART IV

DEVELOPING A PROMOTIONAL STRATEGY

For many people, promotion and marketing are synonymous; the first three sections of this book have demonstrated the fallacy of this view. Simply 'bolting on' a promotional strategy to the existing operations and managerial process is the worst possible approach to marketing. Not only does it encourage a production-oriented perspective, it fails to recognise the right of those the school exists to serve to have their perspective on the school considered. Marketing is fundamentally about looking at an organisation from the point of view of the market and changing the perspective of all those within the organisation to share that market perspective.

Once that fundamental change has occurred it then becomes valid to consider how best to communicate with the market. Promotion encompasses all those activities which enable such communication to take place; this includes:

- informing the market of what the school is offering; and
- persuading the market to take up those offerings.

What makes this task comparatively easy is offering what the market wants; the task of persuading the market to buy a fork is made considerably harder when the market wants a spade! This is where the importance of identifying needs and expressing what the school can offer in terms of benefits becomes clear, since the market might be asking for a spade when the benefits delivered by a fork more closely meet its needs.

In Chapter 10 the most visible form of promotion – advertising and publicity material – is examined, and criteria for selecting media and producing copy and layouts are established. In Chapter 11 personal selling and sales promotion are considered; for most educators these seem the most inappropriate promotional strategies, generating images of second-hand car salesmen and tabloid bingo competitions. Curiously, personal selling and sales promotion are the most commonly used (and probably the most effective) promotional strategies in schools – they are often called 'open days'. The fact that they are not recognised as involving personal selling and sales promotion may well indicate how much room there might be to improve them!

Corporate image has already been introduced as a key factor in the school's position vis-à-vis the market. In Chapter 12 the establishment and management of the corporate image and the institution's public relations strategies are examined. What to do to get a regular pattern of press coverage is only part of the school's strategy; equally important is handling relationships with the media when things go wrong.

Finally, Chapter 13 addresses the perennial question: 'How much should I spend on marketing?' The answer is always going to be equivocal:

- How much are you currently spending?
- What do you want to achieve?

However, this chapter establishes some guidelines to help in answering these questions and, equally important, how to measure the effectiveness of that spending.

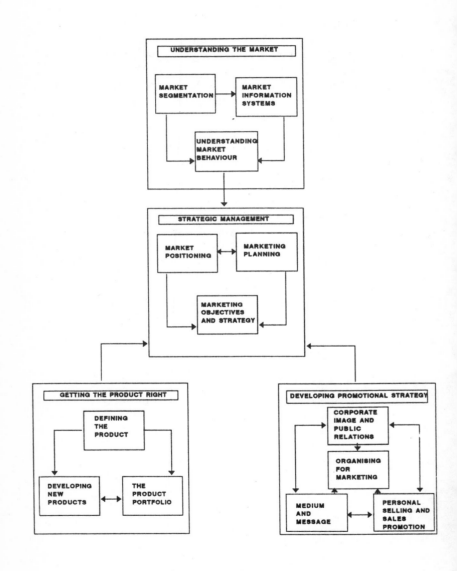

Chapter 10

The Medium and the Message

Legal, decent, honest and truthful?

There is research to show that TV viewers enjoy the commercials more than some of the programmes they interrupt and that glossy magazines without advertising are far less attractive to their readers. However, most people are ambivalent about advertising, though they tend to worry most about its impact on others, confident in its failure to influence their own behaviour.

Yet promotion does have an effect on the market's behaviour; in attempting to understand that effect, the ethics of advertising and publicity cannot be ignored. In general, people find the promotion of washing powder less problematic than the promotion of schools. Why is this? What criteria are to be applied to a product or a sector to decide whether and how it may be advertised or what safeguards must be imposed to protect the market from the blandishments of suppliers? It is one of the curiosities of our attitude to advertising that a washing powder manufacturer is subject to far fewer constraints on its promotion than a GP or a solicitor, although both the latter are already subject to strict ethical supervision of their activities by their respective professional bodies (unlike the former).

The assumption underlying our attitude towards the promotion of certain services stems from the strong ethical dimension of those services. Education, like medicine and the law, is something to which people believe they have rights, and of which they expect certain ethical standards. Advertising, is usually considered amoral, serving the purposes of the organisation using it, whatever the ethics of that organisation or its products. Some would question this amorality; control of advertising by those who have economic power and influence over those who lack such power could be seen as serving a particular morality (or ideology). It is beyond the scope of this book to debate this other than to assert that it is possible to use advertising and publicity to serve a range of purposes. In an educational system which is organised on market principles, it is necessary for schools not only to ensure that they are meeting the needs of their market, but that the market learns that fact and believes it to be true. Schools may not have the resources of large commercial organisations to support their promotional effort but that does not prevent them from making use of the same techniques. Furthermore, it is important that those techniques are used to maximum effect when the resources are so limited and the outcomes so important.

Informing and persuading

It is usual to describe the functions of advertising and publicity as being to inform (to transmit information) and to persuade (to affect behaviour or attitudes). At one extreme, classified advertisements in newspapers serve the former function:

'Secondary school, co-educational 11-18 comprehensive, near town centre, has vacancies for all ages. Applications invited.'

It is unlikely that any school would include such an item in the small ads of their local paper, although many private schools insert small display advertisements which do little more than inform the market that they have vacancies.

Anything more than a straightforward announcement of fact is there to persuade the market to undertake a particular course of action or to alter attitudes towards the school. Simply inserting the phrase 'excellent examination results' in the classified advertisement above will change its emphasis, partly because it includes an overt judgement about the school rather than factual details, but also because such a statement is designed to affect attitudes. After all, if everybody knows that the school has excellent exam results such a statement would have no impact.

Why make this distinction? Because all publicity must have a purpose; the assumption that 'all publicity is good publicity' hinges on the notion that the purpose of publicity is to raise awareness (to inform). But if the purpose is to change perceptions from negative to positive, then bad publicity is worse than no publicity at all. Furthermore, the changing of perceptions is, in itself, of little value if it produces no behavioural effect. Ultimately, all publicity must be designed to produce a particular behaviour, whether through informing, persuading, or a combination of both. Changing attitudes may be an intermediate stage, but the ultimate goal will still be to affect behaviour. This is illustrated in Figure 10.1, which also emphasises the interaction of values and personality with attitudes and their expression through behaviour.

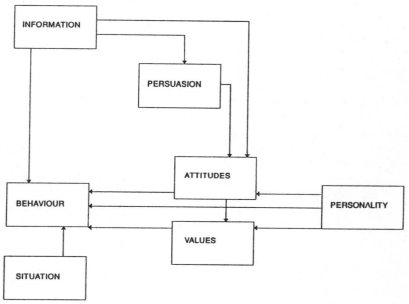

Attitude: a predisposition to respond in a particular way to objects or
               situations.
Values: a hierarchical structure of attitudes.
Personality: the basis of social competence (performance in relation to others) in
               individuals, defined by Eysenck along the two dimensions Neurotic/
               Stable and Introvert/Extrovert.

Figure 10.1 *Information, persuasion and behaviour*

This model is important because it emphasises the key characteristics of the behaviour which it is intended to influence:

- Behaviour is a response to situations; without an awareness of the situation in which the behaviour is to occur it is difficult to influence it constructively.
- Information may be necessary for rational decision-making but behaviour is as much a response to attitudes, values and personality as it is to the outcomes of logical deduction.
- Attitudes (and the value systems of which they are a part) are affected by information and persuasion and by personality. They in turn determine behaviour.
- Attitudes determine how information is perceived and assimilated; it is easier to ignore or reject information which is inconsistent with attitudes than it is to change those attitudes.

What does this all add up to? Where a set of attitudes exists in a particular market segment, regarding a particular school or type of school, changing those attitudes is difficult, and sometimes impossible. Using factual information to counter such attitudes, no matter how valid that information is, will not necessarily change them.

Challenging attitudes head-on is likely to be the least effective way of changing them (and affecting behaviour). It is easier to change attitudes by presenting information and persuading with arguments which fit into the value system of the other (working within their frame of reference). It is better to aim at moving them slowly towards a different perception, with consequent changes in behaviour in the longer term, rather than expecting publicity to produce an immediate and major change in behaviour.

Publicity into action

Publicity materials contain three key elements:

- overall design (layout and graphics);
- a headline, slogan or other attention-grabbing device;
- body copy (the main text).*

*In the case of broadcast publicity, on radio, TV or film, these elements will be found in the visual or aural effects, script, etc. The principles are the same but the practical expression is slightly different.

The purpose should be to generate action; if the publicity is not intended to cause any action then it is questionable if it is needed. Deciding what action is wanted is necessary before any decisions can be taken on wording and design. Action will only result if readers have actually noticed the publicity (it has grabbed their attention); if they have then been encouraged to read it (it has interested them); and that interest has been converted into a wish to take advantage of the product (they desire it). This process:

Attention

Interest

Desire

Action

is a simple yet valuable one to think of in designing and writing publicity (and is easily recalled by the simple mnemonic, AIDA). The visual effect (design, graphics, headline, slogan) should grab the attention and encourage interest, the copy should encourage that interest and stimulate desire; this should lead to action. All too often there is no clear idea of what action is supposed to result, and the effort put into attention-grabbing is wasted. Or, alternatively, a clear action is intended but no effort is put into getting people's attention.

How can this AIDA process best be followed? David Ogilvy (an Englishman who founded a leading New York advertising agency) propounded the theory of the 'unique selling proposition' or USP. No product, however complex, should attempt to put over more than one simple reason to purchase: its USP. The logic for this is that a range of reasons to purchase simply encourages a complex comparison of one product against others. This muddies the arguments and confuses people in making decisions.

Although there are some who reject this theory, most successful publicity tends to focus on one idea and through the use of images and slogans encourages the market to remember, recognise and respond to this. A school which believes it has a multiplicity of reasons to be selected should look for a common theme or concept which links these and use that as its USP. For example, a school which has achieved both academic and sporting success should see these not as two separate messages but as a single reason to select the school: success. The two different routes to success are evidence to support the USP.

The importance of the USP lies not just in the choice of copy but in the way that design (typefaces, colour, graphics, layout, and so on) is used to convey and reinforce the message. The availability of low-cost desk top publishing systems has given many people access to tools to produce technically high-quality publicity materials. What it doesn't do is provide users with the technical skills to design effectively. Using design to convey the appropriate message, to grab attention and encourage interest, is about more than being able to operate the software. Good design can simplify the whole process of communicating the USP and lead the market towards the desired action.

The value of good design lies in its ability to convey a message succinctly and clearly to the reader; one image can be worth pages of copy. Using the design skills and knowledge available to an institution to produce effective publicity is more important than many realise. It is far better to produce a simpler leaflet on cheaper paper if the saving can be invested in a good designer!

The copy should be written to reinforce images; concentrating on benefits, not provision, it should seek to convert the initial attention and interest into a desire for the product and thus to action. Fewer words are always better; shorter sentences rather than long; and simple language rather than obscure terminology and complexity. Compare the following:

Extra-curricular activities:
We offer a full range of extra-curricular activities, available at lunch-times and after school (such as the chess club, netball team, computer club or drama society), and pupils are encouraged through our pastoral service to participate as much as possible.

with

Clubs and societies

Why not learn to play chess at lunch-time or join the netball team after school? You could learn to programme a computer or act in the school play. Your personal tutor will help you decide what's right for you and encourage you to have a go!

The language of the second piece is accessible, the benefits (learning and doing) are identified rather than being hidden, the emphasis is on the pupil rather than the institution, and the philosophy of participation is transmitted without being over-stressed. Perhaps the most important dimension is the use of 'you' and 'your' rather than the use of the first and third person; the message is market-centred.

'The medium is the message'

Marshall McLuhan's famous dictum was based on the premise that the various media of communication each had particular qualities which determined the nature of the communication. While the validity of this assertion has been challenged, it does at least have the merit of drawing attention to the communication channel (the medium) as well as its content (the message) and the interrelationship between the two.

All publicity can be defined in terms of its content and purpose (what it says and is trying to achieve) and its channel. Certain messages can only be communicated by a particular medium, others can appear in a variety; when resources are short and organisations are looking for opportunities to spread the cost of design and copywriting over a variety of different forms of publicity, it is important to think how transferable messages are between various media.

The distinction between publicity and advertising is not particularly important but it is useful to clarify the terminology. All communication with the environment external to the school which affects attitudes or behaviour can be regarded as publicity; in that sense it is an all-embracing concept. For practical purposes it can be thought of as consisting of:

- advertising (publicity in media owned or controlled by others, where space and/or time has been purchased to display it);
- promotional materials (publicity in the form of leaflets and other display formats owned and controlled by the organisation and distributed or displayed by or for them);

- public relations (other forms of communication not intended for display, and media coverage which does not involve payment for space and/or time).

The third of these is dealt with in Chapter 12; this chapter is mainly concerned with advertising and promotional materials; aspects of the latter are also considered in Chapter 11 insofar as they support selling and sales promotion.

Clearly, one important distinction between advertising and other forms of publicity is that it involves purchase of space and/or time in other media. Its distribution is therefore beyond the advertiser's control. This illustrates the importance of the medium to the message since what can be said in the advertisement and how it will be perceived are dictated by the communication channel. Each advertising medium has its own qualities which shape the message, and affect its transmission and its reception; each must be evaluated accordingly.

Newspapers and magazines

Newspapers and magazines are the most obvious advertising media; their selection and use requires advertisers to consider a variety of questions:

- What is the circulation? How many people buy the publication (or receive it if it is a freesheet), and how is it purchased and/or distributed?
- What is the readership? How many people read each copy and who are they?
- How regularly is it published and what are the lead times for advertising? Is it daily, weekly, monthly – and how long before publication must copy or artwork be submitted?
- What is its lifespan? How long is it kept for and read before being disposed of?
- What are the rates per column centimetre for display advertisements and for full-, half- or quarter-page advertisements, particular positions or repeats?
- Does it print in one colour? Are there different lead times for colour? What form should artwork take? (Colour can be two, three or four with the latter giving full colour reproduction)

The advantage of newspapers and magazines is that they are not transitory media; they last and can be referred to during their lifespan.

It is possible to quantify fairly accurately the level and exposure (how many people have seen an advertisement) and its quality (who those people are). The use of reply slips and phone numbers can generate responses to give a measure of effectiveness, although a fairly low response rate (1 or 2 per cent of the readership) is to be expected.

The expansion of local freesheets (newspapers not paid for by recipients) and the increasing sophistication in the production of traditional newspapers and local magazines (such as county magazines) makes it possible to target particular areas by having an advertisement only in those editions being distributed to particular addresses or through particular newsagents.

The disadvantage of such media is that it is usually impossible to avoid advertising to a large proportion of non-members of the market. It would be highly unlikely for a local paper to have a circulation which consisted primarily of parents or potential parents. Most of the cost of the advertising would therefore be wasted, spent on those outside the target audience. To make comparisons between alternative media, it is useful to examine not just costs in total through each, but the cost per market member (see Figure 10.2).

Paper A has a circulation of 12,000 and a readership of 19,500 – of whom 800 are in the target market.
A quarter page costs £175.

Paper B has a circulation of 19,000 and a readership of 32,000 – of whom 1,200 are in the target market.
A quarter page costs £275.

Cost per target reader for Paper A = $\frac{£175}{800}$ = 21.9p

Cost per target reader for Paper B = $\frac{£275}{1200}$ = 22.9p

Although B has a large circulation and a higher penetration of the target market, it costs more per member of that target market although its cost per general reader is lower (£8.59 per thousand as opposed to £8.97 per thousand for A).

Figure 10.2 *Comparing advertising costs*

Posters; transport and bus-shelter panels

Often neglected as an advertising medium, posters offer a relatively low-cost form of advertising. The lengthy exposure and repeat exposure they offer makes it possible to increase awareness substantially. There is little chance of carrying a complex message as the size of the display limits what can be said (other than for large and expensive poster sites). However, regular exposure over a period of weeks or months can be very effective in increasing recognition of a school. The ability to change posters at intervals can be used creatively for 'teaser' advertising – transmitting a larger message by spreading it over a sequence.

Posters and panels do have an additional production cost over and above the design cost, whereas, with newspapers, production cost is contained within the rate; this should not be forgotten. It is also far harder to determine audience exposure for such advertisements, although space-marketing companies will usually be able to provide a fairly accurate indicator of the number and type of people likely to see a particular display.

Broadcasting: radio and TV

It is highly unlikely that a school would consider using TV to advertise itself, because of the high cost and regional spread. It is fair to point out that late night spots can be surprisingly inexpensive; however, their low cost reflects the low viewing figures, and generally they will not offer a high target market penetration.

Radio is a much more attractive medium; local commercial radio has a limited catchment area (its broadcasting 'footprint') and can deliver a very tightly segmented audience. Targeting mothers of young children or children of a particular age is far more feasible with local commercial radio than with some other media, by careful selection of the time for an advertisement to be broadcast. Radio stations are also able to produce an advertisement which, for a simple voice-only commercial, would probably be at little or no additional cost.

The disadvantage of commercial radio is again the wastage, with a high proportion of the audience being outside the target market. It is also an expensive medium and highly transitory; a 15-second slot at mid-morning will be at a standard rate or higher, and will easily be missed. A series of advertisements would be necessary to achieve any impact on the market.

Cinema

The costs of producing a cinema advertisement are high, and using a 'still' with a voiceover is not cheap, although the costs of showing such an advertisement are relatively low. The problem is the audience; the average cinema-goer is a teenager, attractive only to a sixth-form or FE college. However, by judicious selection of timings to match particular films, it is possible to achieve a high degree of penetration of this market if it is appropriate.

Any advertising presents problems for a school; some will object to the principle; others may dislike the message. Certain media are perceived as more superficial than others and it is probable that attitudes towards the principle of advertising a school would be more negative for these. Newspaper adverts will be seen as the most appropriate, posters will not generate too many objections, broadcasting on radio and particularly on TV will cause some alarm and a cinema advertisement would probably generate the most controversy. If the purpose of advertising is to encourage a particular target group to select one school rather than another, controversy may not be welcome!

Promotional materials

Advertising is not the only form of publicity, nor in fact is it the most commonly used in education. Schools will generally rely very heavily on various types of leaflet or brochure and on direct mail to publicise themselves. Various other promotional aids (tee-shirts, sweat-shirts, balloons and the like) are also available, as are exhibition displays (examined in Chapter 11).

Leaflets

The simplest photocopy and the most sophisticated four-colour printed leaflet both have a job to do. A single sheet, possibly folded to make a small booklet, appears easy to produce and attractive as a promotional vehicle. Yet this apparent ease disguises the level of sophistication necessary to ensure it is effective.

All the principles outlined earlier have to be present:

- How does it grab the reader's attention and encourage interest? (Headlines, slogans, layout, graphics.)

- Is the interest converted into desire and does this lead to action? (Selling copy, contact names, addresses, telephone numbers, business reply envelopes.)

All too often a leaflet can consist of little more than a recitation of facts, an outline of the process from the viewpoint of the provider. Thinking about the people in the market, the issues they are interested in and the questions they want answered is the key to success. The use of colour, high-quality printing and paper may help this process; well-written copy and attractive design can ensure it.

Brochures

The brochure – usually described in education as a prospectus – is a larger and more detailed version of a leaflet. A leaflet may be designed to encourage readers simply to seek more information (the intended action); a brochure should be designed to produce applications or, at the very least, visits.

Why the difference? A leaflet is short, and limited in its possible content; a brochure can be as long as is needed to transmit its selling message. If it is impossible to convince the market to take the physical step of visiting or applying to the school without the market requiring more information then a brochure is not fulfilling its purpose.

However, the need for detail does not mean that a brochure is a maintenance manual; it is not intended to tell readers *how* the school operates, but to describe the experiences prospective pupils could have in ways that stress the benefits to them. Images (photographs, line drawings, graphics and so on) can convey many of these benefits far more effectively than words. A picture of pupils receiving their exam results can communicate the success – and pleasure of success – the school offers in a way that text never will.

The disadvantage of brochures is that a high-quality product can be expensive. A cover in colour with monochrome pages on good-quality paper will not be cheap. The higher the volume the lower the unit cost, but for most schools a relatively low print run (a few hundred) does not make this possible. One solution, being used widely, is to have a high quality folder which is used for two or three years (thus obtaining the print run to bring down unit costs) while producing inserts each year in-house. These latter can then be used as leaflets on their own, or combined together in the folder as an alternative to a brochure.

This strategy can be very effective, but it is worth considering carefully how far it is possible to use single-sheet leaflets as part of a larger brochure. The leaflet is often designed to produce a limited outcome (a request for more information, for example). The brochure should answer most questions and for this reason it must have far more detail and should be constructed with care; simply putting a lot of single-sheet leaflets together in a folder does not produce an effective brochure.

It is also worth considering how far the quality of the inserts matches the quality of the folder. If the folder has been printed, in colour, and conveys an image of the institution at odds with photocopied sheets of typescript, it is the latter image which will prevail. There are ways of overcoming this; one is to find a local printshop with a laser or inkjet printer and supply copy on disk. Having it printed out in a high-quality format which can then be photocopied costs very little and adds substantially to the impact. The medium is the message!

Direct mail

Direct mail is used to describe both a distribution channel and a form of publicity material. As a distribution channel it is the most finely targeted medium available, enabling publicity to be delivered to identified individuals. As a form of publicity material it can consist simply of leaflets and brochures or can be designed specifically for the purpose, taking the form of a personalised letter.

Every penny spent promoting the school to those people who will not use it is wasted; eliminating as many of these people as possible is the prime purpose of media selection. Direct mail is attractive because it enables an organisation to decide exactly who will receive the publicity, either by acquiring a mailing list of individuals or by having material delivered to addresses identified as potential 'customers'.

Acquiring mailing lists (from the education authority or from a feeder school) is the easiest way to target the market. A school can also build up its own by recording names and address of enquirers or visitors and noting existing or past pupils with younger siblings. Keeping these records on a simple database can enable personalised letters to be sent by using a 'mail merge' facility with word processing software.

Where a name and address is not available, postcodes can be used in conjunction with the Royal Mail's Household Delivery Service to target particular sectors (an average of 2000 addresses) considered likely to contain the target market. Other door-to-door distribution services will accept even more tightly targeted deliveries, allowing a street-by-street selection.

Being able to personalise a mailing is the ideal; a letter addressed to an individual in an envelope with their name on it is far more likely to be read. Despite people's aversion to 'junk mail' there is plenty of evidence to suggest that, when done properly, it is the most effective medium for publicising services and generating action. The UK market is relatively underdeveloped in terms of direct mail compared to the rest of northern Europe and North America. UK households receive less direct mail and so are able to give more attention to what they do get.

Compared to other forms of printed publicity direct mail relies less on design and more on copy-writing. The letter is a personal medium in which the writer speaks in the first person to the recipient in the second person. A direct mail communication should not say: 'The school can offer its pupils ...' but 'I can offer your child ....' This language has the effect of involving the recipient (who is being engaged in a conversation) and encourages talk of benefits rather than the production process.

Responses to direct mail should also be logged; if a mailshot has invited recipients to an open day, those attending should be recorded. Follow-up letters could thank them for coming and remind them of what they saw and what they could now do. Those not attending can also be targeted, giving alternative opportunities to visit or supplying information they missed. Records of the effectiveness of each mailing can be kept (if there is no identifiable action to be measured for assessing effectiveness, the validity of the exercise itself is dubious). Analysis of the results can then be used to:

- identify potential areas for improvement in the mailing process and materials;
- identify the point at which further mailing is likely to be ineffective.

The example in Figure 10.3 shows just such an analysis. It enables the school to assess how effective each step in the strategy is, and question whether any changes should be made. For example, would sending out a brochure increase more visits at stage 3 and obviate stage 5, which has the least impact?

Method	Response
1 A letter sent out with a leaflet to invite potential parents to an open evening, using education authority mailing list.	
400 letters sent, 150 attendance	37.5%
2 A letter to attending parents inviting them to put their child's name down for the school.	
150 letters sent, 60 applications	40%
3 A letter to non-attending parents inviting them to telephone to make a visit.	
250 letters sent, 25 phone calls	10%
4 A letter to those parents having visited, inviting them to put their child's name down for the school.	
25 letters sent, 20 applications	80%
5 A letter to those not visiting inviting them to put their child's name down, including a brochure (normally given out at open evening or visit)	
225 sent, 5 applications	2.2

Figure 10.3 *Assessing the effectiveness of direct mail*

An integrated strategy

The various approaches outlined above can clearly be used to complement each other, using advertising to raise public awareness, and leaflets, brochures and direct mail to convert that awareness into action. These in turn can be integrated with the various forms of sales promotion and the personal selling outlined in the next chapter. Seeing the promotional strategy as part of the overall marketing strategy is equally important, which means having clearly defined targets for promotion which relate to the broad marketing objectives.

An advertising programme, however limited, which raises the profile of the school and encourages parents and their children to respond positively to it can form one part of that promotional strategy. Backing it up with suitable publicity material ensures that initial interest can be followed up and converted into suitable action.

The school may also want to attract other uses for its resources (meetings, sports and recreational activities, and so forth); it may want to encourage employers to provide sponsorship or offer work-experience placement; it may want to encourage estate agents to promote the school on its behalf. All these objectives can be supported by publicity materials designed for that purpose. However, they should also integrate into the overall strategy. Unless the separate markets can be kept isolated from each other (which is unlikely), any material targeted at one group should correspond with other materials. This is not just important in the design (where a standard format can enhance recognition) but also in the content, where the underlying message is the same. Telling different things to different market segments is always dangerous. The purpose of market segmentation is to ensure that the presentation of the message is appropriate, but not to send out conflicting messages. Only when the products are so distinctly separate (such as promoting facilities for hire out of school hours) is it safe to promote services in a way that clearly differentiates between one and another.

Summary

Promotion is an essential component of marketing and is far more effective when the school has adopted a market-oriented approach. It can then be used to inform the market and persuade them to choose a school which is offering what is wanted. Promotional activity should set out to grab the market's attention, create interest and a desire for the product, and encourage action as a result. This is best done by identifying the key feature which will appeal to the market – the unique selling proposition – and supporting this message through the design and content of publicity material.

The various ways in which publicity is transmitted need to be evaluated for their effectiveness in reaching the target audience and their suitability for the message. Whether advertising by buying space or time in media controlled by others, or by using leaflets, brochures or direct mail within its own control, a school should always determine what objectives its publicity has, and make decisions between the alternative strategies available according to their suitability for the purpose.

Chapter 11

Personal Selling and Sales Promotion

The gift of the gab?

Selling is one of the most under-rated (and derided) of occupations, not readily associated with schools, to which the idea of selling education is often anathema. Selling is seen as persuading people to buy things they don't want, fast-talking sales people confusing and brow-beating others. Selling is superficial and morally dubious.

How valid is this popular mythology? If selling has only a fraction of the dubious characteristics with which it is usually credited, it is doubtful whether it does have a place in schools. Yet the reality is that personal selling does occur: parents visiting a school to decide where their child should attend are shown round and have the school's philosophy and practices explained. They are experiencing personal selling. That neither parent nor teacher would necessarily call it that does not change the fact. Personal selling could be defined as: '*all those contacts between individuals where one party attempts to persuade another to undertake a particular course of action.*'

Contact can be in person, by telephone or in writing, but is on an individual basis; the seller and purchaser address each other, rather than the purchase being part of a group. Thus a direct mailing to a market segment does not fit into the definition, nor does a public address to a group of parents. Some of the principles of personal selling may be relevant to these situations, but they are not personal selling because they are not personalised and are not part of a two-way communication process.

The 'hard sell', the spiel learnt by rota, and the false bonhomie of salespeople, clearly fall into this category but do not necessarily represent the only approach – nor do they demonstrate good practice. Understanding personal selling as being about persuading people to undertake a particular course of action takes us back to Figure 10.1 (on page 175). Action (or behaviour) results from the interaction of a number of factors, including situation, personal attitudes and values, and particular motivations. To influence that action means understanding those factors and controlling the situation so that the individual will make the decisions wanted. Unlike advertising and other publicity vehicles, this is being done on a personal basis. The principles remain the same.

Marketing is about adopting a market perspective – seeing the organisation and its products from the point of view of the market. A major part of the marketing effort should go into finding out about that perspective, whether it be the whole market, particular segments, or particular individuals. Persuading people to behave in a particular way is far easier if they are predisposed to that course of action. Ensuring that the organisation and its products meet the needs and wants of the market is an essential prerequisite of effective marketing. Presenting the organisation and its products in a way that most readily fits the perceptions of the market will then encourage them to 'purchase'.

Personal selling encapsulates all these issues; it involves:

- finding out what individuals want;
- ensuring the product is right for them;
- presenting the product in a way that suits their perceptions and fits their frames of reference, in terms of benefits and not product features;
- enabling them to act in the desired way.

What is important is to start by finding out what they want; those salespeople who start by listing all their product features fail at this first hurdle. Good selling, effective selling, is about listening rather than talking, allowing the customers to say what they want and then providing just enough information and experience of the organisation and product for the customers to persuade themselves to purchase – if the product is right!

The salesperson with the 'gift of the gab', the usual role model, is the example of bad practice, not good. The best salespeople are often the quietest, the ones who listen and plan their sales interviews to produce the best effect. Neither too extrovert nor too introvert, they don't browbeat people into buying what they don't want, partly because it only causes long-term problems and partly because it is far harder than persuading them to buy what they *do* want. Ethics, rather than being alien to selling, are valuable, since they reinforce good practice. Ensuring people get what they want and don't get what they don't want is both right in principle and right in practice.

Selling is communication

Communication is about a message being received as well as transmitted: listening as well as talking. Yet listening is far harder than most people think; it is not enough simply to keep quiet or be passive. Listening is an active process of:

- receiving the message;
- 'decoding' it to ensure it is fully understood;
- responding to acknowledge, confirm and clarify the message.

Simply hearing what is said doesn't necessarily mean it has been received adequately; the messages must be considered and mentally questioned to ensure they are fully understood. This may involve decoding, to read the hidden messages, messages camouflaged behind the speakers' wishes to say what they think they ought to say rather than what they really think. There is also the need to ensure that the language they are using means what the listener understands it to mean.

Reflecting

One technique is to 'reflect' back to speakers what they have said. Reflecting is not the same as repetition – it doesn't mean reciting the speaker's words, but involves:

- summarising what has been said;
- clarifying complex messages by separating confused or interlinked statements;

- establishing priorities in what has been said;
- asking for confirmation;
- steering the conversation in the right direction.

The final point is important: as far as possible reflection should be done in question format, so that the salesperson is not being seen to take over a conversation but to interpolate into it. Having asked a question, the conversation must then pass back to the customer.

Nevertheless, by carefully structuring the interventions the salesperson can ensure that the conversation is steered towards the most appropriate issues. The establishment of priorities through reflection can ensure that customers talk about the things which are important to them and which the school can offer relevant provision for. For example: 'Just to clarify what you're saying then. You want a school that's not too far to travel to or so large so that your daughter will feel overwhelmed, and one which is not too rigid in its discipline. It must encourage pupils to be self-disciplined though, and to take a sense of pride in the school. Most importantly of all, it must encourage them to develop to their own personal capability, whether that's in academic work or sport, or in a vocational area. Is that about right?'

Questioning

Listening cannot occur unless the customer is talking, however, so effective selling depends on good questioning. Questioning is not interrogation, and care needs to be taken not to subject the customer to the 'third degree'. Good questioning should stimulate a conversation and encourage customers to give the salesperson the information needed to understand their perspective.

It is generally suggested that questions starting with 'who', 'what', 'when', 'where' or 'how' are preferable to questions starting with 'why'. 'Why' is a challenging word, suggesting that a course of action or an attitude, belief or wish is of dubious validity. It can be substituted for by questions which are more specific ('Was there a particular reason for ...?') or which address the issue in a roundabout way ('Did you talk to anybody else about it ...?' 'Have you looked at alternatives before deciding that?').

Body language

There are many stories about the problems of Arabs and northern Europeans communicating, with the former advancing and the latter retreating in a waltz-like dance around a room. The problems of non-verbal communication are far more important than many people realise: conventions about personal space, touching, eye contact, hand movements and position, how we sit or stand, are all cultural signals learnt as we grow up and they tell our partners in a conversation as much or more than words do. Telephone communication is far harder than personal communication because it lacks the additional messages conveyed by our bodies which emphasise, clarify and expand our words.

Personal space is that part of our environment which we need to control and preserve to ourselves. The disempowered can have their personal space invaded easily: we will often stand closer to or touch people we see as in need of help (the elderly, the physically disabled) without checking their perception. We would not invade the space of those in positions of power over us; we knock at doors, wait to be asked to sit, don't stand close or rest on their desk.

Establishing personal space is important for ensuring good communication. Holding people at a distance, preserving your own space, or coming too close, invading theirs, is to assert your power. Effective selling requires a rapport between the participants: a mutual respect and understanding. This is best achieved by not trying to establish or enforce inequalities but by demonstrating a concern for their position and showing your wish to communicate as equals. Given the multi-cultural nature of British society, this requires an appreciation of the other's perceptions and expectations, and a recognition that what one person considers an appropriate distance may be seen as aloof and unapproachable to another. An awareness of the issue and a sensitivity to others can easily overcome misunderstanding.

Touching presents a similar set of issues. It is a traditional part of British culture to shake hands as part of a formal greeting or parting; in other cultures shaking hands is a very informal greeting and is practised far more widely. Equally with touching; holding an arm to guide someone, or to emphasise a point may be an unwelcome contact for some people. Care and sensitivity to others will ensure that communication is enhanced.

Maintaining *eye contact* is a far simpler rule to learn; honesty and integrity are always reinforced by eye contact, and *its* absence communicates *their* absence. Liars avoid looking you in the eye; unfortunately those people who are nervous or uncertain will also avoid looking straight in your eye. Effective selling depends on trust; customers must believe the salesperson, and this is best achieved by not evading their eyes.

Obviously, this is only possible if you are face to face; it is therefore problematic when a salesperson is dealing with two or more people. Ensuring that an opportunity exists for face-to-face contact is therefore sensible; talking to each person in turn (rather than flitting from one to one) will overcome the latter problem. (Obviously, care must be taken not to appear to be aggressive by adopting a piercing stare!)

The way hands are moved and held can help or hinder communication. Hand movements can emphasise words; they can also detract from them if they are excessive. There is also a tendency for people to cover their mouths when lying, so that movements of our hands round our mouths can indicate dishonesty. Hands and arms are also part of our general *posture*, the way we sit or stand when communicating. Rapport can be helped not just by the verbal language we use but by the body language. *Mimicking* the posture of those being sold to (by the position of our bodies) will help to establish an effective rapport. This doesn't mean gross bodily stances or movements to copy every one of the customer's, but a slight and casual approach.

Interviews with customers (prospective pupils and parents) which are intended to encourage them to choose a school will be far more effective if the communication process is thought through carefully, and both words and body language are used carefully.

Effective communication, then, depends on the use of our bodies as well as our words to establish a rapport with customers through:

- observing their personal space and avoiding either invading it or using ours to assert power or authority;
- being aware of the impact of personal contact (including handshakes);
- maintaining eye contact;
- avoiding excessive hand movements and hand positions which discredit words (and recognising the significance of customers');
- mimicking customers' posture

Product and customer knowledge

How well we communicate is not just about presentation, it also depends on what is communicated. This means knowing the product and the customer as well as is possible before the sales presentation occurs. The reality is that most managers in schools know the product well; however, it pays to take care particularly where innovations are occurring. (It is also useful to check that a class is not out on a field-trip the day the parent of a prospective pupil comes to see it!) Careful preparation and researching the specific aspects of the product which the customer is likely to be interested in are wise precautions.

Equally, knowing the customer is important; obvious details like their names, where they live, other children at the school hardly need mentioning. But it is also sensible to know what publicity they might have seen, previous visits (to open evenings, for example) and any specific queries they might already have made. This ensures that the customers are aware that you have paid attention.

Knowing the product and the customer makes it easier to identify their likely demands and prepare for them. In particular it means stressing benefits rather than product features; giving reasons to 'buy' rather than technical details of provision. This point has been mentioned many times before but can't be overemphasised. People make decisions on the basis of their wants and needs; the school must therefore be presented in those terms to show how those wants and needs will be met. Effective selling involves selling benefits and being confident that those benefits can be provided through the way the school operates.

Planning sales interviews and setting objectives

Every sales interview should have a clear objective, with one or two alternatives as fall-backs, should it prove impossible to attain that main objective. The objective may be a decision to select the school and enrol next term; it may simply be agreement to come to an open evening.

The purpose of objectives is to give a focus to the sales interview. It also provides a basis for evaluating the sales interview afterwards. The judgement will otherwise be a one-sided impression, using the outcome as the only basis for determining whether or not it was worthwhile, rather than starting with the objective and measuring the outcome against it.

Only having one objective is limiting; any alternative outcome becomes a failure and this puts pressure on the salesperson to achieve it at any cost. Establishing one or two fall-back positions takes the pressure off and enables the interview to be prepared for and structured better. As one outcome appears unlikely to be achieved, another can be introduced and the interview can progress towards a positive conclusion. It may be that a final objective is to ensure that even if the customers are not prepared to choose the school they will go away remembering a positive experience and tell others of that.

It is useful to keep a record of all such sales interviews and a brief note of the objectives and outcomes so that they can be reviewed periodically and any pattern noticed. If this record is filled in before and after the sales interview, with the objectives recorded in advance, it encourages a better-planned approach. Having decided the objectives, it is easier to decide how the interview should be progressed, what should be shown, what materials are needed and who should be met.

This does not mean a heavily formalised system; a simple diary to record visits is adequate. Given that more than one person may be undertaking such an activity it coordinates it and makes it possible to identify follow-up action. For example, if a phone call is to be made to find out the customer's decision, this can be written down on the appropriate day and a record of the outcome kept. The purpose of such a system must be to keep a balance between effective management of the sales process and excessive bureaucracy. Without recording it, however, one of the most expensive parts of marketing (labour time) will go unnoticed, uncosted and unmeasured.

Handling objections

The greatest problem most people have when engaged in personal selling is being able to cope with objections. Objections are either ignored, leaving the customer unhappy, or rejected, leaving the customer *very* unhappy! Yet objections can be seen as positive signals: as they identify those factors which the customer regards as most important.

Objections should not be taken personally; different views about what is important or unimportant should not be taken as an attack on the salesperson. Objections at least show some interest or concern. It is better to have a customer with definite views than one who has none or couldn't care less about the school or what it is trying to do. This is why objections need to be approached creatively, and any opportunity taken to turn them round into positive reasons to 'buy'.

The most important technique for converting objections into positive features is called *reframing;* it involves taking an objection and looking at those aspects of it which might, through redefinition, become benefits. For example, a parent who objects to a school because it has no sixth form (an 11–16 secondary feeding a tertiary or sixth form and FE colleges) might be asked: 'Do you think it's important to have the specialist staff needed for teaching in a sixth form?' It can then be pointed out that the school *has* teachers who specialise – in teaching pupils from 11 to 16 years old. This avoids having sixth form teachers frustrated by having to teach 14-year-olds just to fill up their timetable. (Different arguments would apply, of course, in the reverse situation!) Instead of reacting to the objection, or putting up a counter-argument, reframing of the question allows a point of agreement to be reached, instead of the conversation becoming adversarial. The compensating features (that the staff are specialists in teaching 11 to 16-year-olds) then become easier to advance and to reach agreement on.

Closing

Closing is the final part of the sales interview – converting the discussion into action. It is too easy to leave an interview unresolved, with both sides having different ideas of what should happen next or; worse still is when neither side has any idea! An effective sales interview closes on a positive note, with both sides knowing clearly what commitment has been made.

To close an interview, a salesperson should look for signals from customers that they wish to make a commitment. They may not know what the next step is, or who is responsible for taking future action; they may be looking for guidance on what to do, or some clarification of what the options are. It is important to be alert for these signals and ready to respond to them.

Closing can be effected using a number of techniques; different ones may be appropriate in different circumstances.

The 'alternatives' close

Offering the customers the alternatives open to them allows them to make their decision, or at least to eliminate those options which they don't want. Care must be taken not to exclude options, especially if these might have an attraction, as the salesperson may be seen as trying to exclude an option to reduce competition.

The logical close

This is useful where a series of interconnected decisions have to be made. Customers are led through, each decision following on logically from the last until the final decision is arrived at.

The assumptive close

This assumes the decision has been taken and involves agreeing the action the customers must take as a result. It could involve asking them to sign appropriate forms, or it could involve discussing which class the pupil will (not might!) enter. Such a close can only be used where there is no doubt about the customer's decision or it might rebound painfully on the salesperson!

The interrogative close

This is the most direct: 'So, have you made a decision?' It enables customers to avoid making a decision ('We'll have to go away and think about it,') or to make the decision which the salesperson doesn't want to hear. As a way of closing it removes any control from the salesperson and is also challenging to customers.

However, as a last resort, it is better than having no clear decision at all!

Exhibitions

Exhibitions are an important device for making contact with customers. Unlike a planned sales interview, there is less opportunity to control the process: customers will tend to come through at their own speed and without the salesperson being able to prepare for each one individually. Other than this, the procedures outlined above all apply except that customers are being prepared for en masse.

Exhibitions (which include open days/evenings, careers evenings, and the like) are the opportunity for customers to see what the school is offering and for the school to present itself to a large number of people simultaneously. A few simple rules about exhibitions should be observed if they are to be as effective as possible.

Individuals or small groups should be addressed, not large groups

Collecting all the visitors together and making a speech (or a series of speeches) is an ineffective way of promoting the school. It doesn't allow people to enter a dialogue and certainly isn't particularly customer-friendly. Using several members of staff to provide a more personal interaction is far more effective. This enables the benefits to be spelt out in response to the particular perceptions of the customers, and their objections to be dealt with rather than bottled up.

Personalise the experience

The use of name badges for staff and visitors makes it possible for everyone to know who they are talking to. Addressing people by their name is not only good manners, it makes for a far more effective sales presentation. (This is also true when customers visit a school by appointment. The use of a 'visitor' badge with their name on is a way of encouraging staff to give extra help and it is also a prudent security strategy.)

Support the selling through appropriate materials

Exhibition materials should be simple and to the point. Putting up display panels, or wall mounted-displays, is a way of reinforcing the message being transmitted. The combination of pictorial images and brief headings or short blocks of copy will enable the visitors to receive the images and arguments being conveyed at their own pace. Exhibition displays can be expensive, but producing good-quality materials at low cost is possible.

Colour photographs can be blown up and encased in plastic (heat-sealed) and are a good way of showing what the school does at times or in places when it is not possible to see the school in action. One picture replaces large chunks of copy, and will be seen and remembered where copy isn't. Short blocks of copy, to detail what the school can offer or to explain pictures, should be in large print and as brief and concise as possible. A high-quality effect can be achieved by printing from word processing systems on a laser printer using large-point typefaces. (If the school doesn't have a laser printer, it might be possible to find a print shop or office services company which can do so. Alternatively a friendly local business might do it for nothing. In any case, all that's needed is a compatible system to transfer text by disk.)

A more traditional, but labour-intensive way is to use sheets of transfer lettering rubbed on to paper. This requires less technology, more practice and great care. The paper copy, whatever method is used, can then be mounted on stiff card, cut to size, and used on display boards.

It is also useful to have something for visitors to take away, to remind them of the selling messages and to tell them what follow-up action they need to take. The more material people are given, the less they will read; it is better to produce a few good-quality items than a large volume of low-quality ones.

Promotional items

Promotional items (keyrings, pens, tee-shirts, balloons) are common enough at business exhibitions; how valid they are for schools is debatable. If the school is seen to be giving away materials it may be seen as profligate or superficial, more interested in effect than in supporting good education.

Conversely, the need to attract pupils to ensure the resources to provide a good education requires schools to promote themselves. One approach is to sell promotional items (or at least those worth selling!) so that the school can achieve two goals at once: raising revenue and promoting itself. Supermarkets have done this in the past by charging for carrier bags; schools can sell tee-shirts, sweat-shirts, baseball hats, pens, folders, and the like. Giving away carrier bags with the school logo on to put these materials in can then be seen as a commercially valid strategy.

Sponsorship

Sponsorship serves two purposes for a school: it is a source of revenue and a way of 'borrowing' prestige. A school needs to look very carefully at the way sponsorship can contribute to its operations and its objectives in seeking or accepting sponsorship. Equally, it needs to consider the motivation of those organisations providing sponsorship so that there is no confusion about the joint goals of the school and the sponsor.

Sponsors will fall into two groups:

- those whose purpose is to sponsor certain activities in education for their own ends; and
- those whose purpose is to generate income and/or profits and who use sponsorship to contribute to this goal.

The former will tend to be charitable or non-profit-making organisations with a clear educational or education-related purpose. Their involvement with the school may have a valuable marketing dimension, lending their prestige to the school by association.

The latter's motivation is more complex; the fact that profit-making organisations undertake activities which are superficially altruistic should not confuse schools into misreading their purpose. Such activities are to enhance corporate identities, to raise pupils' awareness of the firm, to encourage pupils into particular careers, to provide a motivating device for their own staff. . . . None of these comments are to belittle such a role; its impact on schools is very beneficial, but in order to get the maximum benefit schools must appreciate why such sponsorship occurs.

Where firms encourage their staff to participate in local community activities they may seek no publicity advantage. It may be done to foster a particular employment climate, encouraging staff to see a large, national or multinational employer as a caring organisation. When a firm offers funding for particular activities or provides learning support materials it may be done to encourage pupils to enter careers in that industry. When a firm runs competitions with prizes which include much-needed computers for schools, this could be linked to a promotional strategy to raise the profile and status of the firm with parents.

Each of these purposes is valid in the context that the firm works in; the school must recognise this purpose and context and maximise its benefit for the school. Approaching a firm for cash or goods to support a particular project in the school with a promise to feature the firm's name and obtain recognition for their role will be of no use if the firm is not seeking such exposure. Emphasising the effect it will have on encouraging girls to pursue science and engineering careers may be far more effective if the firm's key objective is to be able to recruit staff from an adequate future pool of scientists and engineers.

Approaching a sponsor is exactly the same as selling a product: *research the sponsor* to find out what sort of funding they have previously provided. Find out about their operations and products: have any past pupils gone to work in the firm? Keep an eye out for newspaper reports on their profitability so that time isn't wasted on a firm nearing bankruptcy.

Research the sponsorship proposition so that you know what you are seeking funding for. Put together a simple presentation with materials to support it and to leave with potential sponsors to remind them and to enable contacts to show their colleagues.

Set clear objectives for your approach: establish what you are seeking in the way of sponsorship and any fall-back objectives. If a packaging firm won't give money, will it give carrier bags? If a service organisation won't give money, can it supply specialist advice?

Ask questions about sponsorship policies and strategies and listen to the answers, so that the proposals being put can be adjusted to fit the sponsor's objectives. *Don't be offended by objections;* no organisation is obliged to give support nor to agree with the priorities of the school. If a sponsor has a reputation or enjoys a high level of recognition, seeking its sponsorship may mean no more than its agreeing to its name and logo being used. If it is reluctant to do this it does not imply that the school is not fit for it to be associated with, but that it has no reason to offer that association. The failure to provide the reason is the fault of those seeking sponsorship, not the sponsors.

Finally, *be prepared to close:* agree what is being offered and what each party is committing itself to. Ensure that any promotional activities to publicise the sponsorship are agreeable to the sponsor; check what they want to do do to publicise their role. Then when the project or event to which the sponsorship applies has taken place, *review the outcomes* and agree with the sponsor their perception of it as well as the school's. That will ensure that when the next opportunity occurs, both sides know the basis they are starting from.

Customer care

The measure of an organisation's market orientation is the way it treats customers: how their telephone calls are answered and enquiries dealt with; how they are received and treated while they wait; the car parking, refreshments and other facilities they use. Customer care is also about philosophy as well as these practical aspects: it is the market orientation of the school in practice. If all potential pupils and their parents and all those who might influence pupils or parents are thought of as customers and treated as such (without necessarily being addressed as customers) then a school can't help but benefit.

Four simple rules to ensure a high quality of customer care:

- Be accessible.
- Be welcoming.
- Treat everyone as you would like to be treated.
- Demand that everyone else in the school does the same.

Accessibility is about practical matters, and includes direction signs for visitors. Being welcoming means wanting visitors, not regarding them as an interruption to more important things. Treating everyone as you would like to be treated means just that – and setting the highest standards for yourself in the process. Finally, customer care means being prepared to urge everyone else to match those standards; to tolerate bad customer care is to encourage it.

All schools should believe in setting the highest standards in all they do, resources permitting, to ensure the quality of the education they provide. Customer care is one way of showing that to the market; it does not guarantee the quality of the education provided but, given that it is very difficult for the market to experience that education until it has made a commitment to purchase, it is a way of expressing that quality. A commitment to quality in the way a school treats its market in simple things conveys powerful messages about the way it operates and the care it puts into the education of its pupils. As with all aspects of marketing, it is possible to camouflage a poor school by such strategies – but only for so long. In the long term, customer care is not a substitute for quality in education, but an extension of it.

Summary

Personal selling is an integral part of any school's contact with the market; recognising that those contacts involve personal selling focuses attention on the way it is done, and its success. Good personal selling is effective communication, and involves listening far more than talking. Asking questions and hearing the answers ensures that market needs are satisfied.

Salespeople must know what they are selling and who they are selling to, planning sales interviews to achieve predetermined objectives. Objections should be listened to and dealt with, not taken as a personal affront, and the sales interview must be closed so that clear outcomes are decided.

Selling is supported by exhibition materials, including displays and leaflets which emphasise the key selling points. Selling skills can also be applied to obtaining sponsorship, which offers benefits to the school in terms of extra resources and the association with a successful organisation.

Above all else, the school must regard parents and potential pupils as customers, treating them in the way staff would like to be treated themselves. In that way, the ethos of the institution can be made apparent from the first contact.

Chapter 12

Corporate Image and Public Relations

Analysing corporate image

Chapter 2 emphasised the importance of the school's image and market position, pointing out that a school must determine what image it wishes to project and how it intends to establish and maintain that image. This chapter is concerned with just that: establishing an image and then maintaining it.

The image a school has must be backed by reality, but that does not necessarily mean that the market's image reflects that reality accurately. A school must decide what it wants to be before it can set about projecting that through its corporate image. It must also determine what its present image is – how the market sees the school – in order to establish what kind of image shift is needed. This will involve talking to the market (see Chapter 6) and undertaking a critical evaluation of the school and the image it projects.

There are a number of different methods to gauge corporate image. It is possible to ask people to give a brief description of the school, or to choose five words which most accurately reflect it. These descriptions can then be summarised and the views of different market segments assessed. A further variant is shown in figure 12.1: a semantic differential scale with a list of opposing descriptor pairs. Respondents are asked to choose between the pair in each line; by giving the scores to each selection shown along the top and averaging these, an image of the school can be built up.

This checklist is designed to help in the analysis of an institution's corporate image; staff, parents, pupils and other members of the community can be asked to rate the school along each dimension. By scoring each response, a picture of the school can be built up for each market segment.

Question : Please rate _____ school along each of the following dimensions by putting an X in the box which most closely indicates how you feel. If you aren't sure or can't choose, select the central box.

	+2	+1	0	−1	−2	
Traditional						Modern
Innovative						Conservative
Academic						Unacademic
Theoretical						Practical
Successful						Unsuccessful
Conformist						Individualistic
Flexible						Rigid
Disciplined						Relaxed
Friendly						Unfriendly
Businesslike						Homely
Disorganised						Organised
Accessible						Inaccessible
Closed						Open
Warm						Cold
Large						Small
Old						New
Deteriorating						Well maintained
Clean						Dirty
Attractive						Ugly

Figure 12.1 *Analysing corporate image*

The descriptors in Figure 12.1 are not meant to be exhaustive, but to indicate the range of dimensions which can be used. There are very small differences between some pairs (for example, Traditional/ Modern and Innovative/Conservative) but they enable subtle differences to be identified. A school which scores +1.9 on Traditional/ Modern may score +0.3 on Innovative/Conservative. In other words, a very traditional school is seen as being 'middle of the road' between innovation and conservation. It is also possible to analyse separately the images of different groups to see how their perceptions differ, enabling the school to compare its view with that of its pupils, their parents, and so on.

This approach to image analysis is a way of breaking down the complexity of corporate image into manageable elements, with a view to determining how effective the school is in putting across its aims, ethos and style of operation. Where the school is partially successful, it can concentrate on those dimensions where it is under-achieving; this avoids the school mistakenly perceiving itself as having projected a total image successfully, or working on aspects of its image which are successfully established.

Creating a corporate image

Corporate image develops over time as a result of the combined effects of the school's activities, outcomes, promotion and relationships with the public. Creating a positive image can take a lot of time and effort; losing it is easy. One insignificant event can set up a chain reaction capable of destroying a long-established reputation.

Corporate image derives from two sources:

- the generic nature of the organisation;
- the specific activities of the organisation.

A school can't but be seen as a school; that's what it is. It will also be seen as a state or independent school; an education authority or grant-maintained school; a primary, secondary, middle or high school; a comprehensive, grammar (or ex-grammar) school; a coeducational, boys' or girls' school. Each of these has its own generic image: a boys' selective independent school and a coeducational comprehensive start off with dramatically different market perceptions.

On top of this, the school adds its local reputation and history, its physical characteristics and the effect of its marketing effort. A school which converted from grammar to comprehensive ten years ago, set in a leafy suburb with ivy-clad walls, will still be thought of as 'the grammar school' and described as such by the local community. If the school calls its teachers 'masters' and 'mistresses', and they wear academic gowns, and if it boasts every year of its university entrances (particularly to Oxford and Cambridge) it is probable that the school wishes to retain its image.

This does not prevent the school having a highly successful programme for pupils with special educational needs or providing for its less academic pupils; the image reflects the dominant characteristics of the school and cannot cover every detail or nuance. If the school were to abandon school uniforms and academic gowns, use first names for teachers and relax regulations, its reputation for academic success would decline rapidly, irrespective of its exam pass-rates. The market's perceptions are conditioned by decades of acculturalisation and will not easily be dissuaded by facts!

For a school to create a corporate image for itself it must establish two things: what image it currently projects and the image it wishes to project. The former must be further analysed to determine how far it is a product of its generic characteristics (which are largely unchangeable) and how far a product of its activities. The possibility of closing the gap between how it is perceived and how it wishes to be is determined by the impossibility of changing some characteristics and by its commitment to set about changing those characteristics it is able to change.

The less related they are to the everyday reality of the school, the easier it is to change characteristics. Changing a name and logo is very easy; changing a school's culture is very hard. The image of the school is projected through the name and logo and its visual identity, but its basis is the reality of the school; changing the name and logo will not change that reality but can reinforce the reality or create an environment in which change might occur.

Visual identity

Visual identity is a far broader concept than names and logos; it covers the whole range of design applications which the school uses. From the school railings to the school uniform, the school is projecting a visual identity. The name and logo are an important part of it, and are probably the easiest to change, but they are only a part. Nevertheless, changing them is a useful symbol for more fundamental changes, as a way of stressing to the market that the school is now different. Such changes don't need to be large, but they must be significant; the choice between 'high school' and 'comprehensive school' provides the best example. The two descriptors (although educationally they may have no significance) generate different market perceptions. Furthermore, the change of name can be used as a vehicle for obtaining media coverage to make a statement about a more fundamental change.

In choosing a name the school may also choose an emblem to represent itself; this can be a traditional heraldic device (a badge, shield or coat of arms) or it may be a graphic symbol. These are often referred to as logos: graphic symbols used by organisations to identify them and to stimulate public recognition. The effect of a logo is clearly to emphasise modernity rather than tradition, and to create a 'businesslike' image. Some are a compromise, using a graphic symbol but in a badge or shield format, to obtain a balance between tradition and modernity

If a school wishes to use a logo it must recognise that there is more to the exercise than simply asking a graphic designer to 'draw something'. Any competent designer would want to consider the whole set of design parameters relevant to producing a visual identity for the school. These parameters are: the semantics of visual communication; aesthetics; the functional nature of materials and techniques; and economic value.

The semantics of visual communication

'Every picture tells a story': to be precise, every shade and combination of colour, every symbol, choice of typeface and line will create an impression. The way design is used is part of the message being transmitted and that message must be clear, unique (to avoid confusion), simple, visible, legible and memorable. If a school's letterhead or name-board contains a jumble of typefaces, colours and symbols (both the school's and the education authority's) the message it conveys is clear: confusion.

Aesthetics

A design must look good. This means more than avoiding using red and purple together; the overall impression of the visual identity must be aesthetically attractive, and exhibit good taste. Who is to judge what is good taste: the headteacher, chair of governors, or the head of art? It is difficult for many people to accept that others' opinions are more valid, but if the school were judging the physical strength of the sign it would look to a member of staff with the technical proficiency to advise. If the school doesn't trust the aesthetic ability of its art teachers, its corporate image is the least of its problems!

The functional nature of materials and techniques

What will the design be used for? Is it practical (a three-colour design is of little value when the school can only afford single-colour printing); is it visually ergonomic (readable and visible); is it easily reproduced in the various formats required; does it rationalise design (reduce the range of designs utilised)?

Economic value

Good design should be looked on as an investment, not simply a cost; as with all investments, there should be a projected payback to justify the investment. How will the visual identity raise the school's profile, change the public's perception, encourage greater awareness of and interest in the school? In the long run, will more pupils be attracted to the school than would otherwise be the case? This last question is an imponderable, but if the other questions can be answered proactively, it should contribute to stimulating demand. (See Figure 12.2 for a summary of these design parameters.)

Having decided on a corporate identity, most organisations would have a corporate design manual to lay down the rules governing the use of logos, colours and the like. This will establish a house style and provide a specification which others can use to avoid having constantly to refer to a single decision-maker, or to make their own decisions. A school may well feel that this is unnecessary, partly because of the expense and partly because of the limited range of opportunities to make design decisions. Nevertheless, it is worth laying down some principles governing the school's visual identity to ensure standardisation of practices. Such a specification should cover:

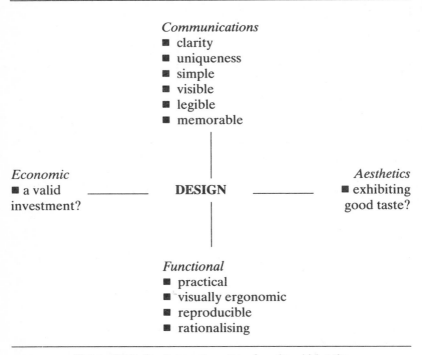

Figure 12.2 *Design parameters for visual identity*

- the typefaces to be used in material for public display;
- the colours to be used for printing and for reference in other media;
- the relative size and position of names, logos, address blocks, and so on;
- the range of situations in which the specifications apply. (For example, should internal decoration all be in standard colours?)

Through the application of such principles it becomes possible to ensure that the school presents itself to the public in a way which constantly reinforces the image the school wishes to project. As corporate design becomes more sophisticated, the public has become more design literate; it expects a standard of appearance from organisations which it may not have done in the past. For schools to ignore this is to let themselves be disadvantaged and to allow negative perceptions to proliferate through comparison with other organisations.

Relations with the public

Corporate identity is one aspect of public communication, the way the school raises awareness of itself and ensures that it is perceived in the way it wishes. In addition to this it needs to ensure that its other communication with the public contributes as well to achieving these goals. This is public relations.

For most organisations, public relations (PR) is just free advertising; when they've got something to tell the market, they hope to 'con' the media into giving them free publicity by sending out press releases which are simply advertising copy in newspaper format. Effective PR is only possible if it is worked on constantly; it incorporates customer care (see Chapter 11) and the development of a coherent corporate identity. It also includes relationships with the local media, local government and central government agencies and offices, social, charitable, sporting, professional and business organisations, and the local community.

Identifying the objectives of any PR plan should be part of the overall development of marketing strategies. PR objectives will need to be coherent to ensure that the same messages are being transmitted to different groups. They will also need to have a strategic focus; PR works on long time scales to have a lasting effect, although it may well do this in an immediate and spectacular way on occasion. Objectives may include:

- building closer links with the community or particular interest groups;
- raising the public profile of the school;
- differentiating the school from others;
- extending the catchment area for the school
- influencing key decision-making groups.

Having established objectives, it is important to establish the timescale in which a strategy is to operate. If the school is due to be considered for closure in three months, the timescale is decided for you. If the intention is to influence future capital appropriations, it may be a five-year timescale with a cyclical emphasis. The PR plan should take into account all objectives, so that two separate campaigns are not allowed to operate in parallel. It should also take into account those events which are fixed in time and predictable – which can be used to gain effect. It is possible to plan substantially in advance with some useful future occasions for gaining press coverage (pupils work experience or exam results) or meetings at which the school will have a presence. Looking for opportunities to fill the gaps in between (or manufacturing them) can ensure that a sustained campaign ensues.

Interest groups (from the chamber of commerce to local charities) provide valuable opportunities to build up the public profile of the school: not just to seek sponsorship, but to contribute to their activities. Offering the school as a facility, encouraging staff to act as speakers, associating the school publicly with events which reflect on it, will contribute to raising its public image. Care obviously has to be taken with political issues, and where staff are participating it is useful to establish guidelines on the conditions when they can speak with the authority of the school. For example, letters to the press or speaking on public platforms can have negative as well as positive repercussions. Staff should know that they are encouraged to participate in such activities but that their identification with the school should be agreed, to ensure it complies with the overall PR strategy.

Ensuring good media coverage is a worthwhile activity but is not easy and should not be approached lightly. It is worth considering how much it would cost to buy a half-page of advertising in a local paper when looking at the volume of press coverage which can be generated by good PR. Equally, the negative coverage which can be discouraged or reduced when things go wrong is worth the effort that might have preceded it over several years. The next three sections look at the techniques of writing press releases and handling crises and, first of all, developing a PR strategy for the local media.

A local media strategy

Who are your local media: press, radio and TV? How influential are they in the catchment area? Establishing which media have the most effect is important – they are the ones to be targeted. How much coverage of your school and its competitors do they give? Is it occasional general features or do they have a specific schools or education feature? Identifying the policy of each media outlet is important since the approach to each must fit into their policy.

When a paper has a circulation area which matches the school catchment area exactly and that school is the only or principal provider in that area, it is possible that a regular weekly or monthly feature could be arranged. This is attractive, but very demanding on the time and abilities of the school to sustain. An occasional feature is preferable, and is more likely to be read by the less committed.

Achieving such coverage, or a lower level of coverage by other media, can involve considerable care and patience. Identify the people most appropriate to approach; invite them to the school for a 'get to know you' opportunity, or for an event which is likely to be of particular interest. Ask questions, about their policy on articles and press releases, their interest in stories on specific educational issues. Read, listen to or view the medium beforehand to find out about it; a paper which has loudly criticised modern teaching methods must be approached with care if your school practises what it has condemned.

Establishing such contacts is valuable with local media; they are likely to be interested in having a 'tame' school to approach, particularly to give a local slant on national or regional stories. If the government has announced a new policy, being able to get a local reaction makes it possible to use such a story in a local paper. Regional papers (and TV) are less likely to be interested in such contacts unless they are based nearby, when the school can offer itself as a 'regional sounding board'.

Local and regional media are likely to be keen on 'human interest' stories, particularly something out of the ordinary. News isn't just bad news; seeing the potential of good news takes some thought but is easily done with practice. A humorous event on your school trip abroad might make a half-page story. Alternatively, even a field trip to the Isle of Wight is news if handled correctly.

Of course, a school trip where something goes wrong is automatically a news story; how badly this reflects on the school depends how well the school has developed its media relations and how well it handles the problem. The latter is dealt with later, but building up a good working relationship with the local press ensures that they will not immediately assume the worst!

Manufactured events (a hot air balloon in the school playing fields or a sponsored beard shaving) are often good opportunities for press coverage. Of course, if every school does it, such events lose any significance; originality and a good press release are the most likely way to get good coverage. A picture opportunity is an added advantage.

Writing press releases

The majority of press releases are badly written and finish up in a wastepaper bin. The media are deluged with them. There are a few simple rules to remember about writing press releases; they are so widely ignored that observing them is likely to get yours included.

Rule 1

News media are looking for news stories. If your press release is not a news story it won't be covered. If your pupils have got the same exam passes as last year, you will be lucky to get a single paragraph at the bottom of a page on a dead week. If one pupil who arrived in the UK as a refugee without speaking English two years ago has managed two passes, that's news. Spotting a good news story is the first step.

Rule 2

Target a press release properly. The appointment of a new head-teacher should be worth a photograph and a single paragraph in a local paper. Sending it out wider than that is a waste of effort. If the school has just appointed a new maths teacher after a year trying to find someone, that could make local TV news and even the daily papers. Suiting the story to the medium is critical.

Rule 3

Keep the story short. Very few newspaper articles, other than in the quality dailies, are very long. What's more, the paragraphs are usually only one or two sentences, without complex subordinate clauses. If the story is worth extensive coverage, the press will investigate it further and obtain any extra details.

Rule 4

Outline the main points in the first paragraph and include the school's name. That first paragraph has to catch the sub-editors' interest to make them read further; it must also catch the readers' interest. A sub-editor may also cut the story, so any important elements must be included in the beginning, since it is common to edit a story from the end, where less important detail will appear.

Rule 5

Identify the source of the press release and any contacts for further

---

PRESS RELEASE

Sir John Smith's School
School Drive
Smithtown
AB1 2CD

Tel: Smithtown (0278) 43106

22nd April 1991

Sir John Smith's School celebrates its centenary
One hundred years after its founding by local industrialist and philanthropist, Sir John Smith, the school which bears his name celebrates in style.

Headteacher Betty Randell has announced a celebration on Saturday, May 4th, which will be the biggest birthday Smithtown has seen. Former pupils from all over the globe are being contacted and visitors are expected from Canada, Australia and Singapore.

Chair of Governors, Tom Peters, whose two children are pupils at the school, is making the largest cake the ovens in his bakery in the High Street will manage. 'Large enough', he says 'to get at least a hundred candles on!'

The school has 680 pupils and is coeducational. In 1973 it changed from a grammar school to being comprehensive and now boasts the highest GCSE and 'A' level pass rates in the county.

Its founder, Sir John Smith, started up his own business from scratch and became the largest employer in the area and was Lord Mayor three times. The original school, a boys-only grammar school, started with 12 pupils in 1891. Sir John died three years later at the age of 78.

For more information contact:

Betty Randell (on 0278 43106)
Sir John Smith's School
School Drive
Smithtown

[Note to editors: The birthday party will take place on the school playing fields or inside the school, if wet, on Saturday, May 4th, 1991. There will be a fair with sideshows, exhibitions of pupils' work, and a reception for past pupils. Photo opportunity.]

Figure 12.3 *A press release*

information. Using headed paper for the first page, with PRESS RELEASE below or opposite the name and address is the simplest way. The name and address of the source should also be repeated at the end with a name and telephone number for the recipients to use for following up the story. If it is an urgent story or the copy deadline is close, giving an out-of-hours number is sensible.

Rule 6

Observe the lay out conventions intended to help sub-editors fit the story to their particular medium. These are illustrated in Figure 12.3.

It is worth checking that each recipient doesn't have a peculiar layout or design before sending them a press release; most will look for materials which observe the following guidelines:

- printed one side only on A4 paper;
- double spaced;
- first paragraph blocked (ie not indented);
- subsequent paragraphs indented (this is known as bookstyle);
- descriptive main heading (don't use clever or punning headings, that's the sub-editor's job);
- no sub-headings;
- clearly dated;
- minimal capital lettering, except for abbreviations (which should be spelt out in full for the first usage);
- no underlining;
- quotation marks for quotations only;
- no full stops for abbreviations (eg BBC not B.B.C.);
- no qualifications after names unless they are pertinent (eg to lend weight to a comment);
- numbers under ten, measurements and signs should be in words not symbols;
- dates written in the form day/month/number (eg Monday, May 6th);
- continuation sheets signalled at the end of each page ('continued' or 'more');
- pages numbered, ideally 1 of 2 / 2 of 2.

Observing these layout conventions and the other five rules will ensure that your story at least gets considered. If the story involves some rather complex educational or technical issue, it is useful to add a 'note to editors' at the end, rather than trying to explain it in the press release. The recipients can judge whether or not to include some explanatory copy. You might also want to restrict publication or broadcasting until after a particular date or time. This can be done by placing an embargo on the release: there is no need to say 'for immediate release' if there is no embargo since this will be assumed automatically.

If there is an event which would provide an opportunity for photography, this should be pointed out. It is also worth providing your own black and white photographs for events already passed; make sure these are properly captioned by attaching a sheet to the photograph which identifies the event, location and participants (by name and role, unless it is a very large group). These need not be sent out with the press release unless the circulation list is small, but their availability should be indicated at its end.

It is also important to keep a record of all releases sent out, their circulation and their appearance in the media. This will ensure that you identify those media most receptive to information and those which aren't. Don't be hesitant to contact both and ask for their advice on the information you are sending. Journalists are generally very happy to comment since well-written and useful information is of more value to them than releases which take up their time for no good purpose.

Finally, don't expect to have blanket coverage of the school in all media; be selective and aim for quality of coverage not quantity. That way, when the really important story occurs, you can feel confident of getting it covered.

Facing up to crises

When roofs don't leak, staff don't go on strike or a pupil isn't seriously injured at school, there is no news. When it does happen, you will find that press coverage is easy to get, no matter how little it is wanted. Crises, big or small, are occasions for publicity even if they are not opportune. Preparing for the worst (even if it never occurs) will ensure that the negative aspects of the event are minimised and the school's reputation isn't seriously harmed (or is even enhanced).

Two major crises during the 1980s provide valuable insights; one was the Bhopal tragedy, the other the Exxon Valdez oil spillage. Bhopal, in India, was the site of one of the world's worst industrial tragedies following an explosion at a Union Carbide factory. The Exxon Valdez polluted large stretches of the Alaskan coast in one of the world's largest oil spills. The reaction of the press and the response of the two companies was noticeably different. Union Carbide had a reputation for effective public relations over many years and immediately set up an information centre to deal with press enquiries. It was very open and provided a substantial body of information.

Exxon (parent company of Esso in the UK) has not enjoyed happy relations with the press; it was criticised for being defensive and for minimising the impact of the spillage, and attempting to avoid responsibility. The reality of both companies' role in the tragedies, the relative geopolitical nature of the events (one in the third world, the other off the US coast) and their practical response to the crisis is not at issue. What is important is to appreciate how perceptions of the organisation affect publicity of crises. A good working relationship, an open response to the situation and a demonstrable honesty can ensure that if a crisis occurs, its public dimension can be managed.

Imagine this scenario: a member of staff has been suspended on full pay following allegations by a pupil. The pupil is known to be unreliable but there is circumstantial evidence to support the allegation. The disciplinary procedures are now in force and the headteacher and the chair of governors will be part of the group considering the case. In this context, neither party must make a public statement in case this prejudices the hearing; the school hopes, by keeping the matter quiet, to resolve the matter without any publicity.

Within 24 hours an article appears in the local paper with full, lurid details of the case and the comment that 'headmaster, Mr Tom Jackson, was tight-lipped yesterday and refused to answer any questions. The chairman of the governors, Mrs Phyllis Baker, 42, a part-time shop assistant, also refused to talk to reporters, fuelling the controversy surrounding the secrecy in this case'! Trite, perhaps, but nevertheless the kind of coverage such a case will attract. A small paragraph six weeks later announcing that the complaint was withdrawn after the pupil admitted lying will not mend the damage done.

How is such a situation to be avoided? The PR strategy for such a crisis must start before it occurs; if the school has had a planned PR strategy, as outlined above, it will have established good relations with the press already. This means the press will trust the school and be prepared to ask for information (and know who to ask).

The school must be prepared for crises by establishing guidelines; one senior member of staff who is independent of the procedures involved must be delegated to handle all press enquiries and all other staff must refer all enquiries to that one person (which means informing staff immediately). A press release detailing the facts, as far as they need to be published, should be prepared. This need say no more than that an allegation (without being specific) has been made and a teacher is suspended on full pay while it is investigated. This should be followed by a detailed explanation of the disciplinary procedures, both to demonstrate the school's openness and to distract attention from the event (where facts are unclear) to the procedure (where facts are not in question).

Any questions should be answered by the relevant person only, and should only be answered in respect of those facts which are in the public domain and which are not subject to debate. In other words, attention should be focused on how the matter will be proceeded with and not the matter itself. Threats should not be used to discourage publication (for example, that the matter is 'sub judice' or that libel proceedings might be undertaken), but the need to discover the true facts by due process should be emphasised.

When the matter is finally resolved, a clear PR strategy to handle the situation should be adopted. If the accusation is found to be unsubstantiated, a simple press release should announce that fact with comment on the relief for the individual and the pleasure of the management and governors that it has been cleared up. If it is substantiated and dismissal has resulted (or a lesser penalty) there might be a need for an informal press conference where the head-teacher, chair of governors and a legal officer are present, with the individual who has acted as the press officer managing the event to control proceedings.

This outline envisages a 'worst case' scenario; any crisis management plan must start from that perspective. It is far safer to tone down such a plan than to try to expand it for a situation far more severe than was envisaged. The assumption that such a situation won't ever happen is only safe to make when it is a physical impossibility, not merely improbable!

Summary

If a school is to manage its corporate image it must start by establishing what image the public currently has of it. It is also important to distinguish how far this image relates to is generic type and how far it is specific to the school. A school can have some impact on the latter but is far less likely to be able to challenge any misconceptions which arise from public perceptions of the former.

The school's visual identity helps to present it to the public; in creating a visual identity, a school must consider what messages are being conveyed and the aesthetics, function and economic value of its visual identity.

Relations with the public also need to be managed as they help determine corporate identity. Planning a strategy to build links with interest groups and the media can help shape its image over the long term. Opportunities for obtaining press coverage should be identified and ensured by using press releases which conform to the six rules. Strategies for managing crises should also be prepared before they occur, so that the school is able to influence any media coverage proactively.

Chapter 13

Organising for Marketing

How much should be spent on marketing?

This is the perennial question, and the answer is always the same: as much as is needed to achieve the objectives set for the organisation. On the surface, not a very helpful response – but it does provide the basis for determining the marketing budget. However, before deciding how much *should* be spent it is wise to calculate how much is being spent now.

The marketing budget is that part of the total school budget spent on the activities covered in the previous 12 chapters. It includes spending on publicity (on advertising, brochures and leaflets, and direct mail), on selling and sales promotion (open days, evenings and the like), on developing corporate identity and on public relations. As well as the materials and services purchased in these activities, it also includes the labour time of staff. This labour time also needs to be accounted for in market research, market planning and product-development activity. The latter may be primarily undertaken through staff-development expenditure and through the normal developmental work of teaching staff, but setting aside even a nominal amount of time (and therefore resources) to focus on market developments is a useful way of encouraging a market orientation.

If all the resources devoted to marketing which have been identified above are defined as marketing expenditure, it becomes possible to see how large a marketing budget might be. Identifying the fact that certain staff might spend, say 5 per cent of their time on marketing activity can cause the marketing budget to be many times the promotional budget, which may currently be the only identifiable marketing expenditure.

Having established, even approximately, the resources currently devoted to marketing, the school should then consider how much needs to be allocated to meet future objectives. In Chapter 3, the process of marketing planning was explained as being:

Where are we now?

Where are we going?

How do we get there?

The first stage involves an audit of the school's marketing activity (which can then be costed to identify the current budget allocation) and the market environment. The analysis of this audit establishes the current situation.

The objectives being set for marketing, derived from the school's mission, provide an opportunity to set specific targets in terms of outcomes before considering how they will be achieved. The third stage is the development of strategies to achieve those objectives; they are not based on how much money is available, but on what needs to be done to achieve goals which are derived from the analysis of 'what can be done' and 'what should be done'.

If this sounds hopelessly unrealistic, it isn't. Resource constraints should not be used to limit objectives and strategies but should be regarded as hurdles which need to be overcome. Only when all resources have been exhausted and they are still inadequate to enable the level of marketing activity desired should the strategies and objectives be reviewed:

- Are there alternative, lower-cost, strategies for achieving the same goals?
- Are the objectives too high to be achieved within existing resource capacity?

Care needs to be taken that the process doesn't become a *post hoc* rationalisation of existing practice:

This is what we currently spend

This is what we currently do

This is what it achieves

This is what our objectives are

In the process of strategic formulation and budget allocation it is important that all options are considered. Strategies and tactics which have always been adopted should not be continued simply because they have always been adopted. Each activity should justify itself against the achievement of objectives; it has to be shown to be effective, and to be more effective than any alternative. Thus the budget-setting process operates in this way:

These are our objectives

This is the most effective way of achieving them

This is what it will cost

It is relatively straightforward to identify those parts of the marketing activity which are invoiced (bought-in materials and services); it is a lot harder to identify those parts which rely on using other budget headings to 'subsidise' marketing. These will include:

- 'borrowed' materials, such as paper, photocopying and so on;
- staff development;
- teaching staff budgets for specialist services and general non-teaching duties which form part of the extra-contractual role (such as open evenings);
- managerial staff budgets for undertaking or overseeing specific marketing activities;
- support staff budgets for undertaking duties which are fundamentally marketing roles.

If it sounds excessively pedantic to insist on accounting for such hidden resources, it is worth utilising a simple convention: ask the question 'if the resource wasn't available from within another budget heading, how would this be done?' If the paper and copying budgets were cut by the 10 per cent spent on producing promotional materials, so that they couldn't be produced, how would promotional materials be obtained? If the art teacher who kindly prepares graphics and layouts were to leave, who would do it instead? The fact that labour is voluntary or extra-contractual does not make it free; if the salaries for the contracted duties weren't being paid, the extra-contractual jobs wouldn't be done.

The lessons of lunchtime duties provide all too vivid an example: once the voluntary nature of the role was recognised and rejected, the school budget had to bear the cost of supervisors instead. Although it may not be appropriate for all voluntary activities to be converted into contractual ones, it is worth identifying those tasks which may be regarded as constituting part of a job role and estimating the level of commitment of time required to undertake it. Other, purely voluntary tasks, may only need a notional cost allocation, but they will at least be accounted for.

In this way a marketing budget can be constructed; the size and importance of marketing for the funding and long-term development of the school can be quantified and thus recognised and managed effectively.

Who should be responsible for marketing?

It is very easy to appoint a member of staff to a role which includes 'marketing' in its job description and think that that means that the school is now market oriented. The difficulty is that this approach tends to separate out those activities which are most overtly 'marketing' (publicity, PR, exhibitions) and need organising by someone with specialist knowledge and skills. It can all too easily cause the other elements – developing strategy, market information and analysis, product management and development – to be overlooked.

The creation of an effective marketing organisation in a school involves defining the marketing responsibilities of all staff, and ensuring that individuals are clear about what they involve and how they fit together with their other responsibilities – and with the responsibilities of others.

The Headteacher's role

Setting the overall strategic direction, establishing market priorities, agreeing budgets and delegating responsibility to achieve clearly defined targets. Above all, the head must demonstrate a commitment to a market-centred approach in the way that decisions are made and strategies developed.

Deputy headteacher's role

Deputies may well take specific responsibility for supervising aspects of the marketing function. A deputy head with curriculum responsibilities will oversee the product portfolio. If the job includes staffing responsibilities, the deputy head should organise development of all staff in marketing awareness, supervise staff with functional tasks (such as writing press releases or organising exhibitions); if it includes financial management responsibility the deputy head will monitor resource allocation to marketing activities and the effectiveness of those activities.

Head of Department's role

Those with a curriculum management responsibility have a product-management and development role. They must ensure that the future direction of the school is supported by appropriate curriculum development and that the driving force behind the curriculum is market orientation.

Teacher's role

Teachers learn to treat the market and marketing as positive features of educational activity, not threatening to their values and behaviour. Equating market orientation with pupil-centred approaches to teaching and learning is the starting point for any staff development related to marketing. The philosophy of market orientation is the nine-tenths of the marketing iceberg which isn't visible; unless it is adopted, the visible aspects are meaningless and a waste of resources!

Administrative staff role

Administrative staff are a valuable part of the marketing organisation, often being the first point of contact between the market and the school. If they are to play an effect part in the school's marketing strategies they have an equal right to appropriate staff development, which includes gaining an understanding of the reasons for adopting a more overt marketing approach and their role in implementing strategies.

Specialist roles

Roles such as PR officer, publicity officer, exhibitions organiser, designer or copywriter – can be allocated according to the abilities and willingness of staff to undertake them. Various members of staff, from the management team down, may take on such roles as appropriate. They should be coordinated by a manager who ensures that targets are understood, resources are available and that activities are interrelated and conform to agreed strategies. This team may be called the marketing team, but it is more aptly named a communications or publicity group.

The real 'marketing team' for a school is its whole staff plus its governing body. Collectively, they are responsible for all its relationships with the market and, more importantly, for the attitudes and behaviours which affect those relationships. Individual responsibilities for aspects of the marketing function should not be walled off from day-to-day activity and marginalised but should be integrated into the operations of the school.

Controlling marketing budgets

In his book *Thriving on Chaos,* Tom Peters identifies ten characteristics which, he suggests, will be essential to the survival and success of organisations in the 1990s (see Figure 13.1). Included in these are the need to delegate responsibility (local autonomy) and for a minimal hierarchy. This means giving staff some freedom to utilise resources to achieve agreed outcomes (not just being able to choose the colour of paper clips). The financial delegation which local management of schools has brought should not stop at the governing body or the headteacher but should accompany the delegation of functional responsibilities identified in the last section. Controlling budgets carefully means agreeing their allocation and the strategy which the budget is there to support, and then allowing subordinates the freedom and responsibility for spending the money and achieving the objectives.

- Flatter (fewer layers)
- Populated by more autonomous units (fewer central staff, more local authority)
- Oriented towards differentiation, producing high-value-added goods and services, creating niche markets
- Quality conscious
- Service conscious
- More responsive
- Much faster at innovation
- A user of highly trained, flexible people as the principal means of adding value

Source: Thriving on Chaos, Tom Peters, Macmillan, 1988.

Figure 13.1 *The characteristics of the successful organisation in the 1990s*

If such delegation is to be effective, it must be controlled – and systems of budgetary control must be established. A marketing plan which identifies not only the marketing objectives and strategies, but also the resources and responsibilities, should have built into it systems for monitoring performance and expenditure and regular reviews. These reviews, related to key stages in the annual cycle, enable outcomes to be evaluated against objectives and budgets to be reconciled (actual and planned expenditure compared).

This process of planning and review provides a mechanism for sharing and delegating responsibility which is an essential requirement if marketing in schools is to be truly effective. At the same time, it builds in checks and balances to ensure that objectives are being achieved and budgets are not overspent. Revisions are then possible if it becomes apparent that outcomes are deviating from plans. Marketing is not a science – it is barely an art form! There are no certainties (hence Peters's title) but the principles of good management apply to marketing as much as to any other area. A combination of careful planning, efficient control systems and a willingness to innovate if circumstances change or the unexpected occurs will ensure that the school's marketing effort is as effective as possible.

Summary

The budget for marketing should not be determined by arbitrary percentages of the total school budget but by reference to the strategies required to achieve the objectives set for the school's marketing operations. If those strategies are necessary for those objectives to be achieved, then the resources they require provide the means for setting the budget. However, all resources should be included; not just the items which are clearly identifiable but also the 'resources' borrowed from other budget headings.

These resources are controlled most effectively by delegating responsibility for them to those who will be involved in achieving the specific marketing objectives. By locating the responsibility for operations and budgets together and setting up clear lines of accountability, management can be made more effective – which means outcomes are more likely to be achieved.

Appendix:

A Skeleton Marketing Plan

A marketing plan exists to give coherence to an organisation's marketing activity, to help manage it and to inform all those involved in marketing what is expected of them and others. It is easy to write a marketing plan as a set of generalisations but this is of no value to an organisation. The marketing plan must be specific, and it must be realistic.

The following guidelines are designed to help a school write a marketing plan. They consist of headings, questions and suggested sources or techniques for producing answers. The value of producing a marketing plan lies not just in the plan itself, but in the insight it gives those involved in writing it into the nature of the school's market and the relevance of existing marketing strategies.

A. Marketing audit ('Where are we now?')

1. Internal audit

Purpose: to examine current marketing and its effectiveness.

a) What objectives are currently set for the current marketing activities which can be identified?
These might be formal objectives, set down in writing in development plans, job descriptions or internal communications. Equally, they may be informal, tacitly agreed and accepted or simply set by the staff involved to give themselves some direction.

b)   How well is the school performing in the market?

The education authority should be able to supply details of numbers of pupils in the catchment area from which market share can be calculated. The greater the detail, the better the understanding of the school's performance. Informal data can also be used, about perceptions of schools, by drawing on staff's awareness of attitudes towards alternatives, which might also be demonstrated in parental preferences.

c)   How is marketing currently organised?

Identify all marketing activity – using the wider definition of marketing and not just promotion activity – and list the staff responsible for managing and implementing that activity. In discussion with these staff, evaluate the effectiveness of the marketing activity, in the light of the answers to A.1.a) and b).

2. External audit

Purpose: to analyse the environment in which the school is operating.

a)   What is the geodemographic profile of the school catchment area?

Identify the geographic distribution of the population in the catchment area, such as proximity, urban/suburban/rural, and so on and the effect these characteristics have on access for pupils.

b)   What is the sociocultural profile of the school catchment area?

This involves analysis of the local population's employment, social class and ethnic mix, to identify how this will impact on demand and attitudes to schooling. Again, information should be available from the education authority and from planning or economic development departments.

c)   What is the employment market like locally?

This involves an evaluation of the potential for employment as well as the structure of the local employment market in terms of the types of job and industry where pupils may obtain employment. The employment market is important to the school – even a primary school – since it enables the school to consider what jobs it is preparing pupils for and the work-experience opportunities likely to be available. The planning or economic development departments and a local TEC or LEC should be able to provide useful information.

d) What alternative providers are there?
Identify principal 'competitors' in both the public and private sector and their provision, market position and marketing strategy.

e) What policies and laws are currently or in future going to affect the school?
As well as changes to the politico-legislative environment which are directly educational in context, it is also important to consider other changes which may have an impact on marketing, such as employment or health and safety legislation which might affect the ability to offer certain provision.

(f) What effect is the labour market for school staff likely to have?
If certain types of staff are difficult or expensive to recruit or retain, the school must consider the marketing impact of this. This may mean adjusting the product portfolio, or it could present future image problems as the school gains a reputation for inadequate staff.

3 SWOT analysis

Purpose : to analyse the data collected in A.1 or A.2.

a) What are the school's marketing strengths from the internal audit?
b) What are the school's marketing weaknesses from the internal audit?
c) What are the school's market opportunities from the external audit?
d) What are the school's market threats from the external audit?

The SWOT Analysis is judgemental and involves evaluating the outcomes of the Internal and External Audits. It is important to strike a balance between enormous lists of minute details on the one hand, and a broad set of headings on the other. The outcome of the SWOT Analysis should be a commonly agreed set of statements about the school and its market which give a reasonably objective appraisal of its current position.

B. Aims and objectives ('Where are we going?')

1. Mission statement

Purpose: to provide a statement of key values and goals for the school which staff, governors/councillors, parents and pupils can understand. The mission statement is there to provide a yardstick against which judgements can be made regarding the purpose of the school.

2. Policy priorities

Purpose: to identify those policies relating to specific aspects of the school's activities which are relevant to its marketing. This may include equal opportunities, curriculum entitlement and similar policy commitments. Identifying them in the marketing plan ensures their consideration and encourages their implementation.

3. Objectives

Purpose: to specify those outcomes of the marketing activity which will contribute to the overall mission of the school and the implementation of policies. To provide a mechanism for evaluating marketing performance.

a)   What quantitative objectives can be set?
Measures of recruitment, staying-on rates, and the like can be viable objectives, but should be set within parameters – upper and lower limits of acceptability. Where revenue is determined by the enrolment of the school, setting clearly defined targets is critical for effective budgeting. This makes it important to set realistic objectives rather than over-optimistic ones which can't be met.

b)   What qualitative objectives can be set?
Measures of attitude change and other qualitative outcomes are hard to set. Furthermore, such objectives are a means to an end – to encourage recruitment – rather than an end in themselves.

Nevertheless, such objectives can be set to identify the route being followed and the basis for judging outcomes determined and agreed, to avoid subsequent argument.

C. Setting Marketing Strategies ('How do we get there?')

1. Product

Purpose: to identify future changes in the product portfolio to meet projected demand.

a)   What product (curriculum) developments are planned?
b)   What is the market rationale for such developments?
c)   Who is responsible for developing them?
d)   What is the development timescale?

Establishing what product changes are going to occur and why and how they will occur focuses attention clearly on the centrality of the 'product' to marketing, and the links between marketing and the curriculum.

2. Price

Purpose: to identify those parts of the school's product range which will be priced, and the principles governing the prices being set.

a)   Will any part of the school's product range be priced?
This includes letting facilities, offering adult education classes, and so on.

b)   What is the purpose of the pricing?
To cover marginal costs, make a contribution to overheads, cross-subsidise other activities and so on.

c)   Will pricing be competitive?
Selecting between low price/high volume or high price/low volume strategies; comparing other providers pricing strategies.

3. Place

Purpose: to identify those developments in the physical location or environment in which products are delivered which may have an impact on the market.

a)   Are any capital developments planned?
b)   What physical maintenance is planned?
c)   What changes in the organisation or utilisation of resources are planned?

Although the school is fixed in place, with the exception of distance learning, it can utilise that place in different ways, and undertake changes in the short and long term to the physical fabric, all of which must be considered for its marketing effect.

4 Promotion.

Purpose: to establish what promotional messages the school wishes to transmit and the mechanisms to be used.

a)   What advertising strategies are to be pursued?
The messages and media, the outcomes expected, the staff responsible and the budget allocation.

b)   What publicity materials are to be used?
The range of publicity materials, their purpose and quantity, the staff responsible and the budget allocation.

c)   What personal selling will occur?
The range of personal selling encounters, their purpose and the staff involved in personal selling.

d)   What sales promotion will occur?
The range of sales promotion activities, their purpose, the staff responsible and the budget allocation.

e)   What corporate image does the school wish to project?
The desired corporate image, how this will be built into promotional and other marketing strategies, the responsibility for developing and implementing strategy for enhancing the school's corporate image, and the budget allocation.

f)   What public relations strategy will be implemented?
Identify who is responsible for coordinating the PR strategy, maintaining external contacts and achieving media coverage. Identify events which will be of PR value, prepare contingency plans for crises and allocate a budget.

g)   What systems will be used for monitoring the effectiveness of promotional strategies and budgets?
Ensure that appropriate systems are devised before strategies are implemented, that staff are aware of the outcomes expected of them and the budgets available, and that reporting times and procedures to compare actual to planned outcomes are known and adhered to.

Index